PLAYBOOK FOR LIFE

A Football Player's Guide to Faith and Purpose

© Copyright Action Takers Publishing Inc 2025

All rights reserved. No part of this publication may be reproduced or transmitted in any form or by any means, mechanical or electronic, including photocopying and recording, or by any information storage and retrieval system, without permission in writing from publisher (except by reviewer, who may quote brief sections and/or show brief video clips in a review).

Disclaimer: The Publisher makes no representations or warranties with respect to the accuracy or completeness of the contents of this work and specifically disclaims all warranties, including without limitation warranties of fitness for a particular purpose. No warranty may be created or suitable for every situation. This works is sold with the understanding that the Publisher is not engaged in rendering legal, accounting, or other professional services. If professional assistance is required, the services of a competent professional person should be sought.

Neither the Publisher nor the Authors shall be liable for damages arising herefrom. The fact that an organization or website is referred to in this work as a referred source of further information does not mean that the Author or the Publisher endorse the information the organization or website may provide or recommendations it may make. Further, readers should be aware that websites listed in this work may have changed or disappeared between when this work was written and when it was read.

Author Email: bwsports87@gmail.com
Author Websites: visit https://bestwishesfoundation.org and www.texasnflflagfootball.com

Publisher Email: lynda@actiontakerspublishing.com
Publisher Website: www.actiontakerspublishing.com

Ghostwritten by Laura Huber

ISBN # (paperback) 978-1-956665-85-7
ISBN # (Kindle) 978-1-956665-86-4
Published by Action Takers Publishing™

Table of Contents

Introduction 1

The Draft: You Have Been Called and Chosen 5
    Chapter 1: Everyone Has a Tag 7
    Chapter 2: Divine Draft 13

1st Quarter: Starting Strong 17
    Chapter 3: Put Me In, Coach 19
    Chapter 4: You Own the Keys 🗝️ 🔑 🍞 25
    Chapter 5: Mind-Blowing Blessings 31
    Chapter 6: The WOW Moments 35
    Chapter 7: The Need for a Father 41

2nd Quarter: Adjustments and Endurance 47
    Chapter 8: Treat Others the Way You Want to Be Treated ... 49
    Chapter 9: Don't Lose Sight of the Truth 53
    Chapter 10: Team Up 57
    Chapter 11: Seeing the Soul 63
    Chapter 12: The Power of Pickleball 67
    Chapter 13: There's a Brighter Day Ahead 71

3rd Quarter: Rise and Respond 75
    Chapter 14: She Gave Me Her Last Dime 77

TABLE OF CONTENTS

Chapter 15: The Power of Testimony 81
Chapter 16: The Power of the Process 85
Chapter 17: Love Everyone, But Don't Trust Everyone........... 89
Chapter 18: The Spark of Encouragement.................................. 93
Chapter 19: Name the Football 97
Chapter 20: Iron Sharpens Iron.. 103

4th Quarter: Finish Strong 107
Chapter 21: It's a Game of Inches... 109
Chapter 22: Discover What's Special 115
Chapter 23: Check the Film 121
Chapter 24: Are You Called to Go or Stay? 125
Chapter 25: The Inner Spirit 131
Chapter 26: Finishing Strong 135

OVERTIME: When It's Not Over Yet 139
Chapter 27: Fifty Plus One 141
Chapter 28: Moving Mountains 145
Chapter 29: Feeding the Wolves 149
Chapter 30: The SWOT Team... 153
Chapter 31: A Super Bowl and a Super Moment.................... 157

SUPER BOWL: Victory in Christ......................................161
Chapter 32: EXTRA, EXTRA, READ ALL ABOUT IT......... 163
About the Author.. 169

To the Love of my life, Beverly

This is our testimony of love, endurance, and divine favor.

The first time I saw Beverly, I knew. I turned to someone and said, "I'm going to marry that girl." She was stunning — I remember thinking, *Wow, that girl is beautiful.* It wasn't just how she looked, though. There was something about her presence that stopped me in my tracks. She was a senior in high school, and I had just started college. We were young (she was 17, and I had just turned 18) but something about her spirit drew me in. From the beginning, there was a peace about her, a strength rooted in love and faith that I admired deeply.

We got to know each other during that time, and it didn't take long before we built a life together. Our first daughter, Brandy, was born in 1984, and then came Blair in 1988. Through it all (college, career, raising children) we remained a team. We didn't come from wealth, and there were times when life was far from easy, but Beverly and I worked through everything side by side. We never broke up, and we never let disagreements take root. If there was ever tension, it never lasted long. I learned early on that a little humility goes a long way. Sometimes all it takes is saying, "You're right. I'm sorry. I love you," and letting her have the last say. Eventually, we always agree on everything.

Even now, all these years later, I can look back and clearly see how God guided our steps. Beverly has always been the glue that holds us together. Her steady support, love, and faith have carried us through more than I can count. She has supported me, encouraged me, and helped raise our daughters into women of strength and character. She also helped shape my walk with God. Her faith was unwavering, and that had a lasting impact on our family and on me as a man.

In 2018, we faced a storm we never saw coming: Beverly was diagnosed with stage 2B Triple Negative breast cancer. This cancer is one of the most aggressive cancers affecting women of color. To hear those words was devastating. We endured 12 rounds of chemotherapy, surgery, 20 rounds of radiation, and six months of an oral chemo as a preventative measure. But Beverly faced it with courage and faith, never wavering. And by her faith and the grace of God — she beat it. She's been cancer-free for over six years now. No Evidence of Disease! We thank God every day for that miracle.

Beverly's healing wasn't just a victory, it was a calling. Out of her testimony came a purpose greater than the pain: **Iam1of8.org**, a faith-driven foundation created to uplift, encourage, and walk beside other women facing the fight. It stands as a reminder that with God, no battle is faced alone and miracles still happen.

When the girls were in college, we always went to see them together. To this day, their friends still comment on how present and supportive we were with our kids in college and beyond. We showed up. We were involved. We stayed close. And that, to me, is part of the legacy Beverly helped create. A legacy of love, faith, and quiet, consistent strength.

This dedication is for you, Beverly. Thank you for being the heartbeat of our family, the strength behind the scenes, and the love of my life.

John 3:16, *"For God so loved the world that He gave His only begotten Son, that whoever believes in Him should not perish but have everlasting life."*

With all my love,

Byron

Introduction

I want to keep this book really simple. And that's just what we're going to do. What you're holding in your hands is a place for you to reflect on life — *your* life. It's a space where every day can have meaning, where your walk with God and the purpose of your life become more consistent, more intentional, and more personal.

Every day is truly important, but some dates seem a bit more significant than others. I was born on Halloween, October 31st, so I always write a note on that day about some of the things that happened.

I'm the eighth of ten kids (seven sisters and two brothers). We were all born at home. The day I was making my entrance into the world, the rest of my siblings were out trick-or-treating. When they got back home, they either thought it was a real trick or a real treat; there I was, another new baby in our household. These little details matter.

Other examples are my dad's birthday, January 6th, and my mom's on October 15th. These are the kinds of dates that stay with you. The ones you reflect on. The ones you write about. The precious moments that will always be with you.

Over the years, I've found myself paying closer attention to dates like these, not just because they mark personal milestones, but also because they often coincide with something bigger, serving many times

INTRODUCTION

as spiritual signposts. Pay attention to patterns and synchronicities; these are the very fingerprints of God himself. I encourage you to reflect on the dates that matter to you. You might find He's been speaking through them all along.

I created this space to tell my story, and to invite you into your own. This is your invitation to journal with me. This is a place for you to reflect on the special moments and highlights of your life, your history, and your family, as I reflect with you on mine. Each story in this devotional journal is a moment in time, a reminder that your life has meaning, and that every day is a chance to grow closer to God. Sometimes all it takes is a verse, a reflection, or a memory. What matters most is that you stay consistent, have the will to do good, and be the best that you can be to yourself and everyone you meet.

When I go into schools and talk to students, or when I do events like Career Day or Read Across America, I look into the faces of teachers and see how much they carry. Thirty students. Nine months. All different personalities. I look at the faces of the children, and I sense the heaviness in their spirit. I see the silent battles they fight, and the storms they carry inside. And I think we all need a way to navigate through the noise and find peace and purpose in the middle of the chaos.

What, then, shall we say in response to these things?
If God is for us, who can be against us? — Romans 8:31

This is where the remedy of faith comes in: Prayer and Scripture.

I always tell people we don't talk about religions and our beliefs much anymore, so find your *banner verse*. Mine is Romans 8:31b — *If God is for us, who can be against us?* Why that verse? I was born on October 31st. I'm the 8th child. The "B" is for Byron. That verse is personal to me. Every morning I speak it out loud. No matter what I'm facing, that verse reminds me I'm not alone. And I know at the end of the day, when I rest my soul, I know God is for me.

- ☐ When you see a Bible verse written like Romans 8:31b, the "b" refers to the second part of the verse, kind of like splitting it into "a" (the first half) and "b" (the second half) for clarity or emphasis. Romans 8:31b means the latter part of Romans 8:31, which is quoted as: If God is for us, who can be against us?

I hope this book becomes a steady place for you and the beginning of a great legacy as you record your thoughts and reflect on your moments with God.

Write your own story in the book of life by owning your days. Find your purpose. And never forget — **God is for you — so who can be against you?**

— Byron Williams

THE DRAFT

You Have Been Called and Chosen

Before the game begins, you've got to know you've been picked.

Every player in the league remembers Draft Day. The waiting. The tension. The call that changes everything. Spiritually, it's the same and God has already drafted you. He's chosen you for a purpose, and this is the season to suit up and prepare. This section is about discovering your identity, aligning with God's calling, and stepping into the life you were designed for. You're not here by accident. You've been called by name.

Jeremiah 1:5 tells us that: *Before I formed you in the womb I knew you, before you were born I set you apart…*

You've already been chosen. God didn't wait to see your performance; He called you before you even knew there was a game to play.

INTRODUCTION

Call to Action

Write down what you believe God has drafted you for. What unique gifts, passions, or experiences has He placed in your hands? As you work through and read this section, spend time in prayer asking Him to clarify your purpose, and then start showing up every day like the person He's chosen you to be.

CHAPTER 1

Everyone Has a Tag

For we are God's handiwork, created in Christ Jesus to do good works, which God prepared in advance for us to do.
— Ephesians 2:10

I got a text recently from one of my old teammates, Sean Landeta. Sean is one of the best punters to ever play in the NFL. He spent over two decades in the league, playing for teams like the New York Giants, Philadelphia Eagles, and St. Louis Rams.

He said, "Byron, I'm coming to town this weekend."

I told him, "Sean, I can't meet you this weekend; I'm headed to Texarkana. It's my football camp weekend."

I explained to him that we do the camp every year, the weekend after Father's Day.

Why?

Because a lot of these kids don't have fathers.

So we step in.

We come to remind them of who they are. We tell them, *"You're not forgotten. You have been given a tag by God."*

That's not just a phrase — it means something.

Your **TAG** is your:

- **Talents**
- **Abilities**
- **Gifts**

Every person has a TAG. Whether you grew up hearing it or not. Whether you believe it or not. You didn't show up on this earth by accident. You were tagged by God to do something that matters.

Take James "Shack" Harris, for example. He was the first Black quarterback to start a season opener in the American Football League (AFL) or NFL, doing so with the Buffalo Bills in 1969. In 1974, he became the first Black quarterback to start and win an NFL playoff game while with the Los Angeles Rams. He was also the first Black quarterback to play in and be named MVP of the Pro Bowl.

Shack grew up in Monroe, Louisiana, during the 1950s and '60s. It was a time when segregation was still the law of the land. His father was a minister and furniture maker, a hard-working man who taught James the value of showing up and doing your best. His mother was a devout Christian who raised the family in a local African-American Baptist church. It was the backbone of their community and a source of strength in a world that often pushed them down.

James' family history, like many African-American families, carried the weight of slavery and generations of struggle. Their faith and unbreakable spirit were passed down to James "Shack" Harris and became the foundation for his character.

When James got his shot at playing quarterback in the NFL, he faced more than just the pressure of the game. Even though his teammates accepted him, some coaches and executives doubted him, not because of his skill, but because of his skin color. Many fans were not pleased with a Black man on the team they worshiped. Some were skeptical, while others were even hostile. He wasn't paid what others made, making only about half of what his white peers were making at the time. But he didn't let any of that stop him from accomplishing what God sent him to do.

Even though he had to prove himself every single day, James Harris kept showing up. He kept playing like he belonged until there was no question that he did. He was paving the way for every Black man that would come after him.

He was tagged for greatness, and he answered the call.

His story is proof that your TAG isn't about fame or fortune. It's about walking in the purpose God gave you even when no one else believes in you yet. It's about staying faithful when the world doubts.

We all carry something special: a unique talent, ability, or gift that we were born with. Whether you're called to football, farming, music, business, art, or teaching, it's been placed in you and designed by God.

I'll never forget what one young man told me after one of my camps.

He said, "Mr. Williams, I came to your football camp, but I ended up getting a baseball scholarship. The things I learned at camp, I used them in baseball."

That's what it's all about.

Sometimes, you show up thinking it's about one thing, and God uses it for something greater.

You may not be doing what you thought you'd be doing, but you're still walking in purpose.

Your TAG may not be loud, but it's there. And it's valuable.

Don't hide it. Don't downplay it. Don't wait for someone else to validate it. Sometimes, life makes us forget what we carry deep inside. And that's the reason we show up and do these camps. It's to remind young people of the greatness inside them.

Some of these kids will go on to play football. Others may find their lane in baseball, in engineering, or in driving a truck. Every job is important. We're not trying to preach everyone into the NFL; we're trying to help them discover their purpose.

Maybe you don't feel like you have a gift. Maybe no one ever told you that you do. But if you're still breathing, you still have a TAG.

Maybe you're not playing under stadium lights. Maybe you're not getting paid millions. But your TAG is real. Your talents, your abilities, your gifts (no matter how hidden) are yours to own and use.

So, what are you going to do with your TAG, because **you've been tagged for greatness.**

For this reason I remind you to fan into flame the gift of God, which is in you... — 2 Timothy 1:6

Reflection Prompt

- What's your TAG — your unique Talents, Abilities, Gifts?
- Have you been using it, or have you set it aside?
- Who in your life needs to be reminded that they have a TAG too?

Prayer

Father, thank You for the gifts You've placed inside of me. Help me to walk boldly in my calling and to recognize the TAG You gave me from the very beginning. Give me the wisdom to help others discover theirs. Let my life reflect the purpose You planted in me.

In Jesus' name, Amen.

Pause and Ponder this Scripture — Identity & Purpose

There are different kinds of gifts, but the same Spirit distributes them. There are different kinds of service, but the same Lord. — 1 Corinthians 12:4–6

Byron Williams Annual Football Camp

In the Headlines

CHAPTER 2

Divine Draft

For the gifts and the calling of God are irrevocable.
— Romans 11:29

It wasn't long ago when I was watching the NFL Draft and people were calling me to ask for my thoughts on it. It was then that I realized the Draft reminded me of something deeper. For those who are listening to that still, small, inner voice, there often comes a moment when you realize — you've been chosen, not by accident, but by Divine Design.

Not by chance. Not by circumstance. But by Divine Appointment.

You don't need to hear your name called on national television to know you've been selected. God has His own draft board. And when He calls you, it's not about hype, it's about purpose.

In life, just like in football, it matters who's in your corner. You've got to be linked up with the right people, the right environment, and most importantly, the right calling. It's not just talent that gets you to the next level, it's alignment.

Divine alignment is when your gifts, your experiences, and your relationships all begin to make sense because they've been leading you somewhere all along. God doesn't waste anything. To prepare you, He uses every team you've been on, every city you've lived in, every detour you didn't understand. To grow you. To connect the dots.

Sometimes, your vision, your faith, your passion isn't visible to others right away. But when it's your time, God will open doors no man can shut. He will place you exactly where you're supposed to be, and you'll realize everything that once felt random was actually strategic.

I've learned that it's not about being picked early or late; it's about being picked for the right reason in the right season. It's being put on the right team with people who align with you and your vision for the future. You might not have the perfect stats or pedigree, but when God selects you, He equips you. It's not about the crowd's approval; it's about Heaven's assignment.

I believe everyone has a Divine Draft moment. A time when you're called up, not just to do more, but to become more. To take the gifts you've been given and step into a bigger game, a higher level, a sacred responsibility.

That's when you stop asking, "Why me?" and start saying, "Send me."

Because when you know He called you, you stop needing validation from those who didn't.

Reflection Prompt

Have you felt God drafting you into something greater lately? Are you resisting the call because it doesn't look the way you expect? What dots from your past is God now connecting?

Prayer

God, thank You for choosing me — for seeing something in me that I can't always see in myself. Thank You for the divine alignment that has led me to this moment. Help me to trust Your timing and step into the assignment You've drafted me for. Remove any fear, doubt, or distraction, and align me with the people and purpose You've prepared. I don't want to sit on the sidelines of my calling. I'm ready. Use me.

In Jesus' name, Amen.

Pause and Ponder this Scripture – Calling

Before I formed you in the womb, I knew you, before you were born, I set you apart... — Jeremiah 1:5

1ST QUARTER

Starting Strong

The opening whistle has blown — how you begin sets the tone.

In the first quarter, there's energy. Fire. Momentum. But it's also where nerves can get the best of you if you're not focused. This section is all about foundations: prayer habits, mindset, purpose, and discipline. It's about starting strong in your faith walk, not just with hype, but with humility and heart. Champions don't just show up; they show up prepared.

Proverbs 16:3 reminds us to,

> *Commit to the Lord whatever you do, and He will establish your plans.*

The first step of a champion is surrender. Let your plans start with prayer, and your purpose will follow.

Call to Action

Pick one habit to commit to for the next four weeks — something that strengthens your spiritual foundation. Whether it's prayer, reading Scripture, or encouraging your family daily, start strong, stay consistent, and let God build on that momentum.

CHAPTER 3

Put Me In, Coach

Therefore, encourage one another and build each other up… — 1 Thessalonians 5:11

It was gold.

That's how I describe what we did at David Daniel Elementary Academy of Math and Science in Grand Prairie, Texas. The school was struggling, averaging just a 68 percent across the board in 3rd, 4th, 5th, and 6th grades. They needed a boost, and that's when we stepped in with a program we called **Put Me In, Coach.**

We showed up wearing our jerseys, not just to represent where we'd been, but to show the kids where they could go. We were former athletes who played at the highest levels and now we were walking into classrooms with a message: you matter, your attitude matters, your effort matters, and your future is worth investing in.

In our program, the teachers became the coaches, and the students were the players. We started to shift their mindset. I told the kids, "Even though you've already put on your clothes every morning, you've got something else you need to put on — your attitude. You've got to put on your attitude, too."

Winston Churchill tells us that, "Attitude is a little thing that makes a big difference."

We handed out t-shirts, new shoes, and chips, not as bribes, but as tools to build morale, unity, and purpose. But more importantly, we gave out belief. The kind of belief that changes the way a kid sees themselves in the mirror. We made them feel seen, like they mattered, and they responded. We wanted these students to see school as a place they belonged, not just a place they had to be.

We knew that everyone needed to work together to make a change: teachers, principal, counselors, and students — all of us.

Then we came back to the school and threw a pizza party with the students to reinforce what we were teaching — teamwork. Being submissive and respectful to the teachers and waking up every morning with the right attitude. We wanted to drive home the fact that this is a team, and we're in this together. If you get better, the school gets better.

And it worked.

The school that once hovered at a 68, struggling to meet standards, rose to a 93, surpassing expectations and setting new ones. This was not just an improvement; this was a transformation. The STAAR test scores reflected what we already knew: when you change the environment, you change the outcome. And more importantly, the students started believing in themselves. They saw that when *they* got better, the school got better, and when the school got better, the community got stronger.

My work with schools didn't start in the classroom. It started with my business, installing track and turf for schools, and through that, I saw what was happening on campuses across the state. That's when the door opened. God was calling me to do more than just lay the foundation for the field; I got the chance to help lay the foundation for a child's life.

Through my nonprofit, **The Best Wishes Foundation**, I've been able to carry this mission into schools across Texas, from elementary to high school. We bring that same energy and the sports-themed mentorship programs that teach kids to show up, stay focused, and dream big. Doing this helps remind them: *You matter. You've got potential. And you're worth the investment.*

One moment I'll never forget was the time after passing out new shoes, one kid looked up at me, holding his new shoes, and said, *"Coach, this is the first brand-new pair I've ever had."* That's when I knew we weren't just giving out shoes. We were giving out dignity.

That's what *Put Me In, Coach* is all about. It's not about the scoreboard. It's about the soul. Giving every kid the confidence to say, "I'm ready. I belong. And I've got something to give."

At the end of the day, it's not just about football, or shoes, or test scores. It's about testimony. That's what's powerful.

You can learn more about what we do at **bestwishesfoundation.org**.

Reflection Prompt

- Where in your life is God calling you off the bench and into the game?
- Is there someone who needs your encouragement today?
- Think about the ways you can be a "coach" to someone else — by calling out their potential, showing up, and speaking life into them.

Prayer

God, thank You for calling me into the game and for believing in me even when I didn't believe in myself. Help me to show up with heart, courage, and purpose. Use me to lift others, to speak life, and to remind someone that they matter. Make me bold enough to say, "Put me in, Coach," and faithful enough to follow where You lead.

In Jesus' name, Amen.

Pause and Ponder this Scripture – Encouragement

Let us consider how we may spur one another on toward love and good deeds. — Hebrews 10:24

Best Wishes Foundation

BW Sports, LLC in the newspaper

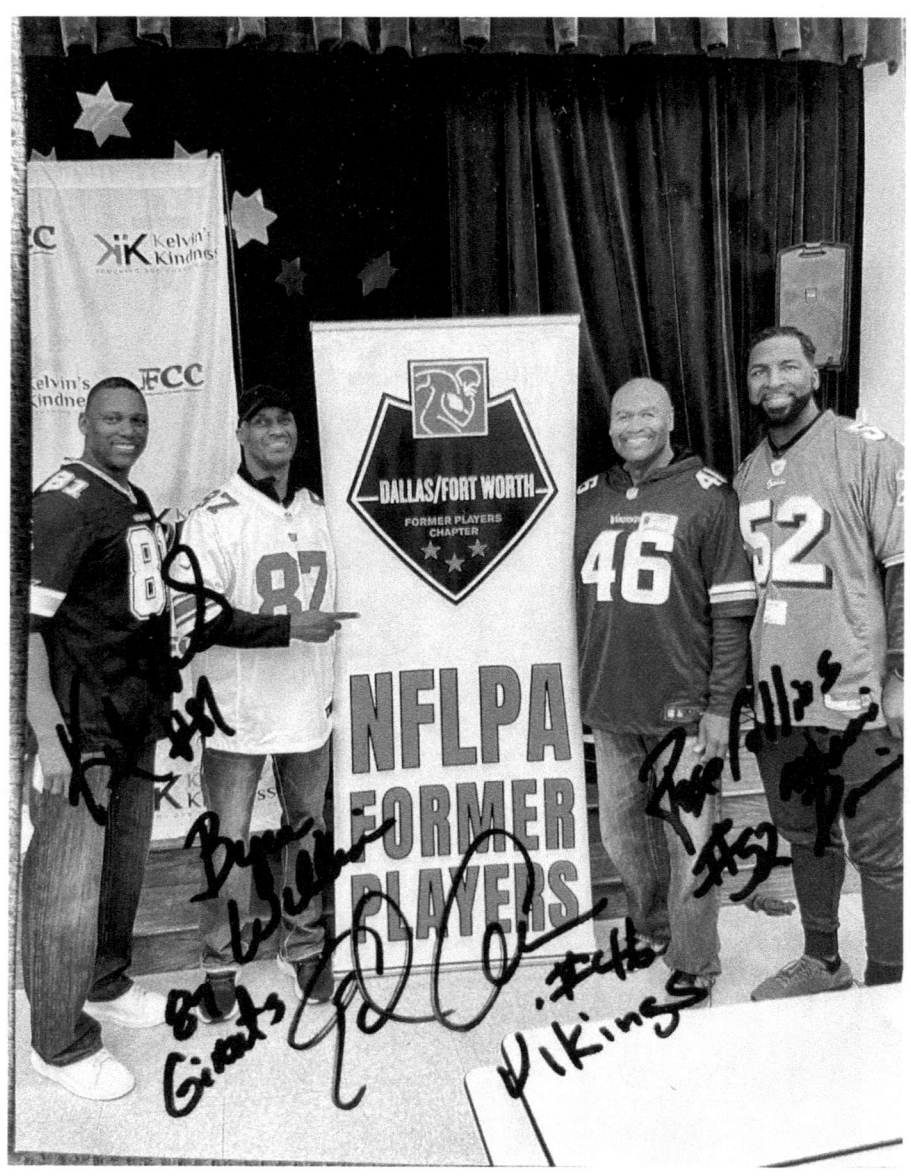

Byron Williams with Kelvin Edwards #81-Cowboys kelvinskindness.org; Alfred Anderson #46-Vikings; Rose Collins #52-Dolphins

CHAPTER 4
You Own the Keys

And I will give you the keys of the kingdom of Heaven; whatever you bind on earth will be bound in Heaven, and whatever you loose on earth will be loosed in Heaven.
— Matthew 16:19

I wanted to drive so bad when I was a little kid. So when I was five years old, my dad started teaching me. I'd sit on his lap while he worked the pedals, and we'd cruise around together. I still remember how his hands guided mine on the wheel, how calm and steady he was. But it wasn't just about driving, he used those moments to teach me not just how to steer, but how to be decisive, directional, and never get distracted.

He'd say, "Look ahead. Don't just react. You have to plan your next move and be decisive," or "Know where you're going before you get there." He was showing me how to be directional in life, how to choose a lane and stay in it. He made it clear I had to focus and that *distraction can cost you everything* — behind the wheel and in life.

YOU OWN THE KEYS 🔑 🔑

By the time I was 14, I drove him all the way to Dallas. That wasn't just a road trip; it was a turning point in my life. I felt trusted, capable, and in control. It gave me the confidence I still carry, because in that moment, I knew my dad believed I could handle the responsibility even if the rest of the world might not have agreed. And more importantly, I proved to myself that I could do it. That's the kind of confidence a father passes down, not just in how you drive, but in how you move through life.

That lesson stayed with me. And over time, I started to see that driving was more than a skill — it was a metaphor for what every young person needs from a father.

A father can give his son or daughter a car, which is a beautiful machine, symbolizing freedom, opportunity, and a gateway to the future. But what if he hands over the car without the keys? They can look at the car, admire it, even dream of all the places they could go but they can't start the engine. They can't experience the thrill of the ride or learn how to handle the road. The car sits there, idle and locked, a blessing that remains out of reach.

If the person receiving the car has never driven, there are other keys besides the physical ones that must come with the car, or the recipient will not even know how to make it run. It's not enough to simply hand over the keys and say, "Good luck." One must be taught how to operate the vehicle, drive responsibly, how to read the road signs, how to anticipate danger, and how to control the vehicle in difficult conditions. The driver must learn patience, discipline, and respect for the rules. Without this training, the car could become a weapon, too fast, too powerful for an unprepared driver, leading to accidents and regrets.

Without guidance, freedom can feel like chaos. But with a father's instruction, it becomes purpose.

This is the challenge many of us face in life. God's blessings (whether they come as gifts of talent, opportunities, relationships, or provision) are given to us with incredible intention. Yet, without the keys to unlock those blessings, they can feel like heavy burdens instead of joyful gifts. The keys come in the form of God's Word, His promises, and the wisdom that flows from a relationship with Him.

The Bible holds the keys to our lives. It gives us the power to start, the guidance to steer, and the knowledge to avoid the hazards that would otherwise cause us to crash or get stuck. Without it, we may have everything we think we need but find ourselves powerless, directionless, or trapped in fear and confusion.

When we neglect those "keys," we risk misusing what God has given, causing harm to ourselves and others. We might speed recklessly through life, make careless choices, or become overwhelmed by the very gifts meant to uplift us.

However, when we embrace these spiritual keys, something amazing happens. We begin to enjoy our blessings in ways we never thought possible. The car that once sat idle becomes a vessel of adventure and growth. We learn to navigate life's twists and turns with comfort and confidence. We move forward with a purpose, knowing that God is our guide and protector.

This is why it's so crucial to seek God daily, to open His Word, and to pray for His Spirit to unlock the understanding we need. It's not just about having blessings — it's about having the wisdom and tools to steward them well. The keys to spiritual growth open doors to peace, joy, and fulfillment that no material blessing alone can provide.

Does it feel like you lost the keys to your spiritual life?

Are you unlocking the blessings God has given you?

Or are those blessings parked, waiting, unused?

Don't let fear, doubt, or neglect keep you from driving the life God has prepared.

When it comes to spiritual growth, many people wait for someone to unlock the door for them, waiting on a perfect moment or a lightning bolt from Heaven to give them clarity. God didn't just give you access. He gave you authority. You own the keys to growth. You own the keys to peace. You own the keys to purpose. It's not locked up somewhere with the perfect pastors or spiritual experts. It's in your hands.

The truth is: you already have the keys.

With God's keys in hand, you're equipped to drive with purpose, passion, and peace. These keys are freely given to you because God loves you and wants you to thrive, grow, and fulfill the destiny He has planned for you. In the book of 2nd Peter, chapter one, verse 3, he says, "His divine power has given us everything we need for a godly life through our knowledge of Him who called us by His own glory and goodness."

Don't just stop at reading, though. Prayer is the engine. It invites Heaven into your daily life. When you pray, you're not just talking to God. You're also unlocking clarity, power, and peace. You're activating the Holy Spirit, who takes the truth of Scripture and applies it to your own decision-making process. That's how spiritual growth happens. It's not magic; it's movement. And the more you practice it, the more natural it becomes.

The cornerstone of your life must be Christ. Everything else has to be built around Him. Your job, your ambitions, your family, your fears — it all has to sit on top of the foundation He laid. That's why I love that my church is called *Cornerstone*. Because that's who Jesus is — the cornerstone (*Built on the foundation of the apostles and prophets, with Christ Jesus himself as the chief cornerstone. Ephesians 2:20*), the solid rock on which everything else is secured.

So don't just show up to church. Engage.

Don't just crack open the Bible when things go wrong. Crave it like your life depends on it because it does.

Don't underestimate the power of prayer and holy Scripture; they are the key to unlocking supernatural direction.

And don't forget the power of the Church. The Church isn't just a weekly gathering; it's a key God gave you to grow, connect, and be sharpened by the testimonies and wisdom of other believers. Don't leave that key on the shelf.

You've been handed what you need. The Bible is your keys and your map. Prayer is your line to the Commander. The Spirit is your guide. And the Church is your crew. **You own the keys.** Don't sit in the parking lot on purpose with the engine running. Open the door. Walk through it.

Grow into the man God created you to be.

Reflection Prompt

- What area of your life have you left locked because you forgot you already have the keys?
- Are you depending on your own understanding, or leaning into the Word and prayer for guidance?
- What would change if you treated God's Word like your greatest resource instead of your last resort?

Prayer

Father, thank You for trusting me with so much. I don't ever want to take that lightly. You've given me everything I need to grow, but sometimes I forget to use it. Stir my hunger for Your Word. Teach me to lean on the Holy Spirit, and to pray with boldness and expectation. Help me grow in maturity and stop waiting for someone else to unlock my future. Give me the courage to start using the keys You've already placed in my hands. I want to grow. I want to lead. I want to reflect You. Show me where to start, and keep me going. Teach me to handle the freedom You give with wisdom, humility, and boldness. May I grow into the person You've always seen in me.

In Jesus' name, Amen.

Pause and Ponder this Scripture – Keys to the Kingdom

So I say to you: "Ask and it will be given to you; seek and you will find; knock and the door will be opened to you." — Luke 11:9–10

Byron's father - Columbus Williams - PFC U.S. Army - World War II

CHAPTER 5

Mind-Blowing Blessings

My son, do not forget my teaching, but let your heart keep my commandments. — Proverbs 3:1

I'll never forget fifth grade. My youth football team was called the Packers. That name would eventually come back around for me, even though I couldn't have imagined back then what it would mean later in life.

Years later, after playing ball at UTA, I got drafted into the NFL by the Green Bay Packers.

It wasn't an easy road. In the tenth game of my final college season, I broke my ankle. That injury nearly took me out of the draft conversation completely. I remember thinking, *Well, there goes my chances.* The dream was slipping through my fingers.

But God wasn't done with me. Even though I was picked in the tenth round — number 253 overall — I got the call from Bart Starr himself. That moment? It was nothing short of *mind-blowing*.

Back then, the NFL Draft had only 12 rounds. There were only 28 teams in the league. Each team had just 48 players on the roster. And there were about 80 players trying out for the teams. That meant competition was fierce, and making a team was no easy task.

There was no room for error. But somehow, even with my injury, I made it. God opened a door I didn't even think was still there. Maybe one of the reasons I didn't let it bother me was because I had a poster hanging on my wall that read:

Trust in the Lord with all your heart and lean not on your own understanding; in all your ways acknowledge Him, and He will make your paths straight. — Proverbs 3:5–6

That verse was my daily reminder to trust God's plan, even when I didn't understand it.

This experience taught me something that continues to shape how I live and lead today. Sometimes, when life seems discouraging or depressing, when it seems like God said "no" to your hopes and dreams, there's actually a divine plot twist in motion. What feels like rejection is often just redirection. And when you least expect it, the blessing comes — not just as you imagined it, but far greater than you could've hoped. That's what I call a mind-blowing blessing.

I've learned that what looks like rejection is sometimes protection or preparation. In those moments, I remember the words from Isaiah 55:8–9,

---

"For my thoughts are not your thoughts, neither are your ways my ways," declares the Lord. "As the heavens are higher than the earth, so are my ways higher than your ways and my thoughts than your thoughts."

What I've seen over and over again is that God's detours lead to destinations I never could've imagined.

Looking back on my life, I see more than ever how important it is to stay grounded in faith — to pray, to reflect on Scripture, and to walk in obedience even when the outcome isn't clear. Eventually, you will see the blessings; it might be a month or a year later sometimes, but the blessings will always come. God always knows just what we need at the time.

I'm currently pursuing my leadership certification, and I know I've been called to help others find their way. Especially young men trying to navigate the road ahead. Leadership starts in the heart — in the decisions we make when nobody's watching, and in how we respond when life doesn't go our way. I believe it's in those moments, when we choose to trust God and stay faithful, that He reveals the most powerful parts of our purpose.

If you're facing disappointment right now, if something didn't go how you hoped, don't give up. Take a step back. Pray. Reflect. God might just be setting you up for something *mind-blowing*.

Reflection Prompt

- Think back on a time when life didn't go your way.
- How did it shape you?
- Can you see a moment where God turned what seemed like a "no" into a bigger blessing?
- Are you open to trusting Him even in uncertainty?

Prayer

Lord, thank You for the divine plot twists in my life — for the times You said "not yet" or "not this way" and turned it into something better than I imagined. Help me to trust You, even in the hurting and the waiting. Remind me that Your plans are always greater than my own. Open my heart to see Your hand in every detail, and guide me with wisdom and peace.

In Jesus' name, Amen.

Pause and Ponder this Scripture – Divine Direction

I will lead the blind by ways they have not known, along unfamiliar paths I will guide them… — Isaiah 42:16

Byron Williams - 62 yd touchdown

CHAPTER 6

The WOW Moments

This is the Lord's doing; it is marvelous in our eyes.
— Psalm 118:23

Sometimes God moves so clearly, so quickly, so personally… all you can do is say, "Wow."

That's a WOW Moment.

WOW Moment

1. A sudden and awe-inspiring experience of God's blessing or intervention that evokes wonder and gratitude.

2. An instance when divine timing and personal obedience converge, resulting in a powerful witness to God's presence and guidance.

3. (Acronym) Wonder. Obedience. Witness. — The key elements that define these moments of spiritual revelation.

THE WOW MOMENTS

Mind-Blowing events are something more dramatic or redemptive in hindsight, while WOW Moments are more about the awe in the present. It's when you experience God's **wonder** in real time — a moment you've prayed for, or didn't even know you needed. When your **obedience** lines up with His perfect timing. And when you're a living **witness** to something that can't be explained any other way but God.

From time to time, I think everybody experiences a WOW moment. Maybe God leads you out of danger, revealing to you that he's always with you, that he's guiding you, that He's directing your path. Maybe you win the lottery. Maybe you meet someone who is just the right person you needed at the time. You get the job. A podcast speaks new life into you after feeling indifferent for a while. A great idea comes to you that shifts everything. Feeling peace in the middle of chaos. There are countless experiences that could be considered a WOW moment.

Many times the blessings in our lives are not what the world would consider huge, dramatic blessings. Sometimes they show up quiet and lowkey. But every now and then, they go big. And all you can say when you're experiencing them is, "WOW!"

I'll never forget the day I got the call saying I was going to receive the *Presidential Lifetime Achievement Award.* I wasn't expecting it. I wasn't campaigning for it. I hadn't been chasing recognition. I was just doing what I felt called to do. But God was orchestrating something behind the scenes. All I was doing was being consistent — showing up, serving my community, speaking when invited, mentoring young people whenever I could. None of it felt grand or award-worthy. It just felt like obedience.

Then, out of the blue, the phone rang. On the other end was Dr. Beverly Kee, a woman who has spent her life quietly and powerfully honoring those who serve. She's the Executive Director of the organization that helps select recipients for national service awards like the *President's Lifetime Achievement Award*.

She also happens to be the sister of legendary gospel singer John P. Kee — a man whose life is a testimony of God's redemptive power. John was struggling and battled addiction, but he turned his pain into purpose. He cleaned up his life, started choirs that reached thousands, and became one of the most respected voices in gospel music today. That's a WOW moment on its own.

I listened to Dr. Beverly Kee over the phone as she told me I was receiving the *Lifetime Achievement Award* for contributing to this great country of ours.

But on this call, I thought to myself, Dr. Beverly Kee wasn't talking about John. She was talking about me.

She said, "Byron, you're being recognized by the President of the United States for giving over 4,000 hours of service, for helping children and adults rise up and become their best."

I was stunned. My whole body went still.

"Wait! Is this for real?" I asked her. "Is somebody playing a prank on me?"

She laughed gently and said, "No, Byron. This is not a prank. This is real."

In that moment, my mind ran back through all the years of unseen effort — the silent work, the thankless hours, the times I questioned if I was really making a difference. And then it hit me, clear as day:

WOW, God. That was You. Every step. Every seed. Every ounce of service mattered. And now, my country is confirming what God has seen all along.

That's the kind of moment you don't forget, not just because it's big, but because it's holy. It's evidence that when you walk in purpose and obedience, God keeps the receipts. He sees what nobody else saw. He remembers what you forgot. And when the time is right, He rewards it.

WOW Moments remind us that God is always placing people, timing, and resources in the right spots to remind us: He's still involved. He's always with us. He's still doing marvelous things.

And here's the real secret: the more you recognize them and are grateful for them, the more they show up. Because God's been doing marvelous things all along. We just needed to pause and pay attention to reap the benefits.

So when that unexpected honor of a WOW moment arrives... When someone you served in silence comes back to say "thank you." When a door opens that no man could've unlocked for you... Let your heart say it before your mouth even catches up: **WOW, God. That was You.**

Reflection Prompt

- What's one WOW Moment you've experienced recently — something that made you stop and feel God's hand on your life?
- How did it shift your perspective or encourage your faith?
- Are you creating space to notice and remember these moments?

Prayer

Lord, thank You for the moments that stop me in my tracks — the divine surprises that remind me You're always at work, always moving, always near. Help me stay faithful in the little things, knowing You see it all.

Let me never grow numb to Your wonders, but instead stay in awe of Your goodness.

In Jesus' name, Amen.

Pause and Ponder this Scripture – Divine Surprise

The Lord has done great things for us, and we are filled with joy. — Psalm 126:3

Presidential Lifetime Achievement Award

CHAPTER 7

The Need for a Father

Do you see a man skilled in his work? He will stand before kings; he will not stand before obscure men.
— Proverbs 22:29

I grew up in a house packed with girls. There were eight of us kids, and my brother was the oldest — he had already moved out when I was born. That meant it was just me and all the sisters (*I wouldn't get another brother for six more years*). My dad didn't think it was right for me to sleep in the same room with the girls, so every night, I slept with him.

And I loved it.

There was something about being that close to him, about having that safety and strength right beside me every night, that gave me a sense of grounding I couldn't have put into words back then. I adored my father. He was a military man, disciplined, sharp, always carrying himself with quiet authority. But to me, he was more than just a soldier.

He was the man who held our house together, who made things work even when we didn't have much to work with.

We lived in a really small house with no plumbing — no running water. But what we did have was love. And my father's vision.

When it came time to move out of that little house and into something better, my dad decided to buy a house that was only a frame. He was going to finish our new home with his own hands. He was a carpenter, and I was right there with him, every single day after school. I'd drop my books and head over to see what my dad was doing. I was just ten years old, and I wanted to learn everything I could from him.

I watched him work, day after day — measuring, sawing, hammering. I didn't realize it then, but those times became the blueprint for how I would live my life. He taught me the value of hard work, of showing up consistently, and of taking pride in what you build, even if no one else ever sees the effort behind it.

He didn't talk a lot, but I learned more in the silence than I ever could have from words. He showed me how to work with my hands and to be proud of what I build.

He didn't just teach me how to build a house. He taught me how to build a life and become a man.

And as I grew older, and the world handed me bigger stages and bigger checks, I never forgot those memories of working beside him. Every time I lay a foundation (whether in football, business, or life) I think back to that little house and that quiet man with calloused hands and a heart full of grit. I realize now, my father wasn't just building a home. He was building a son.

The statistics of having a strong and present father figure in a child's life are nothing short of incredible; they consistently experience better outcomes across nearly every area of life:

- Academically 43% more likely to earn A's.
- 33% less likely to repeat a grade.
- Emotionally and behaviorally show fewer signs of depression.
- Have higher self-esteem.
- Are 75% less likely to become teen parents.
- 80% less likely to end up in jail.

I remember one time I went to visit my daughter at college. She was supposed to come meet me, but her roommate's boyfriend that was driving wouldn't bring her by my hotel to see me. That didn't sit right with me. I found out he was a member of the Texas State football team, so I went straight there. I walked out onto that field, looked him in the eye, and told him, *Don't you ever keep my daughter from seeing her father again.* I let him know that if he disrespected her like that one more time, he'd see me again, and it wouldn't be nice.

See, it wasn't about being tough. It was about showing my daughter she's worth being protected, and showing that young man what respect looks like. As fathers, as men, it's our job to set that tone. Your daughter needs to know you've got her back, and young men need to know she's not alone in this world.

And just like our daughters need to be protected, our sons need to be guided. They need to see what it looks like to be a man, not just someone who's strong, but someone who's steady, respectful, and responsible. A boy without a father will look for manhood in all the wrong places — on the streets, in locker rooms, in music videos, or from peers who are just as lost as he is. But when a father shows up, leads by example, and corrects with love, that boy grows into a man who knows who he is. He doesn't have to prove himself to anybody, because his father already showed him what being a man really means.

Father involvement also contributes to stronger social skills, better peer relationships, and improved self-regulation. In terms of long-term success, children with active dads are more likely to attend college, maintain steady employment, and avoid poverty, substance abuse, and risky behavior. Even when a father doesn't live in the home, the quality of the relationship matters greatly, proving that meaningful engagement, not just physical presence, makes the difference.

Reflection Prompt

- Think about the people who showed you what it means to work with honor.
- What are you building today that reflects the tools they put in your hands?
- If you had a father or strong male figure in your life, how did their presence shape your confidence, character, or ability to overcome challenges?
- If that presence was missing, who stepped in — and how did their guidance impact the path you walk today?
- How are you now choosing to show up for the next generation, knowing that a consistent, loving presence can change a child's entire future?

Prayer

Lord, thank You for fathers who work not just for their families, but with them. Thank You for the strength, wisdom, and quiet leadership of men who pour into the next generation one nail, one lesson, one sacrifice at a time. Help me honor that legacy with the way I live and lead.

In Jesus' name, Amen.

Closing Scripture

The righteous who walks in his integrity — blessed are his children after him! — Proverbs 20:7 (ESV)

Byron's Family in front of the house his father built after it was initially framed

2ND QUARTER

Adjustments and Endurance

The defense is hitting back. Now what?

By the second quarter, you've seen some action, and you've also taken a few hits. This is where adjustments matter. In your spiritual life, this is where you learn to respond, not just react. Prayer deepens. Trust is tested. You learn that God is not just with you at kickoff — He's with you in the grind. This section helps you lean into His voice when life doesn't go according to plan.

When speaking to the Galatians (6:9), Paul tells us,

"Let us not become weary in doing good, for at the proper time we will reap a harvest if we do not give up."

When you hit resistance, don't retreat — dig in. God's got a harvest coming for those who endure.

Call to Action

What needs adjusting in your life? Identify one area where you've been coasting or getting hit hard — then invite God in. Make a practical shift this month (a schedule change, a conversation, a mindset reset) that helps you stay in the fight.

CHAPTER 8

Treat Others the Way You Want to Be Treated

Fathers, do not provoke your children to anger, but bring them up in the discipline and instruction of the Lord. —
Ephesians 6:4

My dad was a military man. Steady. Disciplined. A man of purpose who worked for the Red River Army Depot in East Texas. He gave everyone in our family nicknames. Mine was "Coot." Don't ask me why — that was just my name in his eyes, and it stuck.

But what stuck even deeper than the nickname was the lesson he repeated often: "Coot, treat people the way you want to be treated."

That was his code, and it's a principle I carry with me to this day. It's more than a cliché. It's a life compass. And paired with my mom's words, "There's a brighter day ahead," it gave me a foundation that I still stand on.

Those two sayings remind me why I live the way I do. Why I try to carry hope and kindness wherever I go. Because of them, I understand the deep need in this world for guidance, for compassion, for fatherhood.

This morning, as I was reflecting on what it means to be a father, Ephesians 6:4 came to mind. It says:

And you, fathers, do not provoke your children to wrath, but bring them up in the training and admonition of the Lord.

That's not just Scripture, it's a footprint, a reminder that we're not called to perfection as parents, but to be present, to have patience, and to have purpose.

We live in a world starving for godly fathers. The kind who lead by love, who discipline with gentleness, who live what they preach. Fathers who treat everyone, especially their children, the way they would want to be treated.

As parents, we are the first sermon our children ever hear. And they don't just listen; they watch.

From potty training to teaching respect… from bedtime prayers to hard talks about life… we are the vessels God uses to bring His Word to life for the next generation.

There's no greater influence on a child than the consistent, faithful presence of a godly parent. And there's no greater legacy than to leave a footprint that points to Christ.

Reflection Prompt

- What did your father teach you — by words or by example?
- What legacy do you want to leave for your children or those you influence?

Prayer

God, thank You for the fathers and father figures You've placed in our lives. Raise up more men who lead with integrity, love, and grace. Help me be a vessel of Your presence in the lives of the next generation. Whether I am a parent, mentor, or friend, may I leave a godly footprint that leads others closer to You and helps them to remember to treat people with respect, the way they themselves would want to be treated.

In Jesus' name, Amen.

Pause and Ponder this Scripture — The Golden Rule

So in everything, do to others what you would have them do to you, for this sums up the Law and the Prophets.
— Matthew 7:12

TREAT OTHERS THE WAY YOU WANT TO BE TREATED

Byron's Son-in-Law and grandsons

CHAPTER 9

Don't Lose Sight of the Truth

Then you will know the truth, and the truth will set you free. — John 8:32

Coach Reed saw something in me, and he called it out. He said, "Byron, I will make a deal with you. If you make the A-B Honor Roll every six weeks, I will give you $20." He gave me purpose when I didn't yet see it in myself. That small moment of validation changed everything.

So now, every time I stand before a room full of young people, I try to pass that moment forward. I hold up a $20 bill and ask, "Who wants this?" Some hesitate. Some doubt I'm serious. A few smile and wait.

Eventually, one person steps forward, bold enough to reach for it. But instead of giving them the real $20, I slip a fake bill into their hand.

That person returns to their seat, and I say something like, "Everyone give it up for Johnny, who was brave enough to come get it!"

Then I ask the person holding the $20 bill, "Look closely. What do you see?"

Almost every time, they soon realize it's fake. They always walk back up and receive the real $20. Mostly every time afterwards, a student asks, "Do you have another $20?" I laugh and say, "Yes, but today I'm only passing out one," because Coach always said if you earn it, you will always remember how hard you worked for the reward.

And then comes the lesson. I tell them:

That's life. Life will hand you distractions that look real. It will give you false promises and temporary fixes. Bad influences can be dressed up like golden opportunities.

But the key is to stay focused. Keep your eyes locked on what matters. Even when life fools you, keep showing up. Keep reaching. And in time, you'll be handed something real.

That $20? It's a tribute to Coach Reed. Because he saw value in me before I saw it in myself. And now, I carry that forward, teaching kids the value and power of making sure they make decisions based on truth.

Reflection Prompt

- What are you reaching for right now?
- Is it the real thing — or a distraction in disguise?
- Take time to reflect on the people and paths that are shaping your choices. How can you refocus your mind and heart on the things that last and truly matter?

Prayer

God, thank You for the people who saw something in me when I didn't see it myself. Help me to stay focused on what's real, and not be fooled by things that only look valuable. Strengthen my spirit to keep reaching, especially when I'm tired or discouraged. Keep my eyes on You, the true prize.

In Jesus' name, Amen.

Pause and Ponder this Scripture – Discernment

Look straight ahead, and fix your eyes on what lies before you. Mark out a straight path for your feet; stay on the safe path. Don't get sidetracked; keep your feet from following evil. — Proverbs 4:25–27

CHAPTER 10

Team Up

For where two or three are gathered in My name, I am there among them. — Matthew 18:20

In the NFL, no matter how talented a player is, he can't win games alone. A perfect spiral means nothing without a receiver on the route. A running back can't get to the end zone without his line holding the defense. Even the greatest quarterbacks rely on timing, protection, and trust. Teamwork isn't optional; it's survival. And the same is true in life.

God never meant for us to run solo. We weren't meant to walk out our calling alone. From the very beginning, He embedded the power of togetherness into the faith walk. Jesus didn't send His disciples out solo; He sent them two by two. Not just for backup, but for belief. Not just for strength, but for **spiritual presence.**

He sends us out in twos, surrounds us with witnesses, and places people in our lives to sharpen us, cover us, and remind us of our mission. You need a team. Your purpose is too big and the battle too real to go it alone.

That's what our opening scripture, Matthew 18:20, reveals.

When two or three gather in His name — He shows up.

Not might.

Not could.

He will be there.

That's the power of partnership. That's the difference between surviving and thriving.

Even Jesus chose to work with a team, and he could have done it all alone. He built a crew. He sent His disciples out in pairs. Why? Because there's strength in numbers. There's accountability when one stumbles, and there's credibility when truth is spoken in unity. That's why Jesus said,

---

"Let every matter be established by the testimony of two or three witnesses." — Matthew 18:16

It's not just about friendship. A team isn't just people spending time together. It's individuals walking in alignment, united by purpose, sharpening one another for the mission ahead. Real teams hold each other accountable, speak truth in love, and stay focused on the bigger picture because the goal is too important to get lost in isolation.

When you team up with someone who shares your values and your vision, your strength multiplies. Think about this: a single horse can pull 8,000 pounds, but two horses together can pull 24,000. You would think that if one could pull 8000, then two would pull 16,000, double the weight. But instead, they pull triple the amount. This is because when working together, horses distribute their load more efficiently, making it easier to overcome resistance. This creates a greater overall pulling capacity than individual strength. This teamwork is called synergy.

That's what happens when God joins the gathering.

This isn't just good advice; it's a survival strategy.

If the enemy can isolate you, he can weaken you.

But when you've got someone covering your blindside? A brother praying over your family? A teammate reminding you of your mission when you get off track? That's when the enemy gets nervous.

Think about Paul and Silas. They were arrested, beaten, and thrown into prison for preaching the gospel but they weren't alone. *They teamed up.* And what did they do while shackled in the dark? They prayed and sang hymns *together*. That's the power of partnership. Their faith didn't shrink because of pressure; it expanded because it was reinforced. And what happened?

Act 16: 25-26 says:

The prison shook.

Doors flew open.

Chains fell off.

If Paul had been alone, the song might've never been sung. The prayer might've never been prayed. The breakthrough might've never come. But when two men team up in faith? *Miracles happen.*

You need men in your life who get it. Men who pray, men who study, men who aren't afraid to be vulnerable and hold each other accountable.

Every man needs a team.

In football terms, it's like Joe Montana and Jerry Rice. Individually, they were great but together they were *legendary*. What made their connection so unstoppable? Timing. Trust. Repetition. Respect. Each man did his part with excellence, and they brought out the best in each other. Rice didn't try to play quarterback. Montana didn't try to catch passes. They *stayed in position*, and because of that, they made history.

You don't win alone.

You don't grow alone.

You were made to walk out your life *with* others — people who hold you accountable, challenge you to rise, and don't let you settle.

Find your team. Link arms. Cover each other's blind spots. Push each other forward. Because when two or three walk in unity under God's assignment, Heaven moves.

Team up.

Show up.

Lock in.

That's how men of God get things done.

Reflection Prompts

- Who are the "two or three" in your life that you can gather with in Jesus' name?
- What would change if you were more intentional about building spiritual community?
- Are you allowing isolation to dull your faith — or are you inviting people in to sharpen you?

Prayer

Lord, I don't want to walk this road alone. I know You designed me for community, for brotherhood, and for accountability. Help me to recognize the people You've placed in my life to walk with. Help me be open, honest, and willing to both lead and be led. Surround me with men of integrity and faith — men who will help me pursue You with everything I've got.

In Jesus' name, Amen.

PLAYBOOK FOR LIFE

Pause and Ponder This Scripture – Brotherhood

Though one may be overpowered, two can defend themselves. A cord of three strands is not easily broken.
— Ecclesiastes 4:12

Byron's Parents Columbus & Lorene Williams

CHAPTER 11

Seeing the Soul

There is neither Jew nor Gentile, neither slave nor free, nor is there male and female, for you are all one in Christ Jesus. — Galatians 3:28

One of my most cherished memories goes way back to second grade in East Texas. This was a time when schools were just beginning to integrate, and I had my first white teacher, Miss Tidwell. She was more than just a teacher. She had a way of noticing things about you that others might easily overlook.

I remember how she loved to come by when we were doing our writing exercises. The letters of the alphabet were hung across the classroom, and I would carefully print each letter just like the cards showed. She would walk down the aisle, stop by my desk, pick up my paper, and say loud enough for everyone to hear, *"Look at how Byron wrote his letters. This is the way you should do it."* Then she'd glance down at me, smile, and say, *"You have the best penmanship I've ever seen."*

Those words might sound small to some, but for me they were huge. Her encouragement made me feel a sense of worth and pride deep inside that lifted me up. More than that, it changed how I saw people and how I would carry myself for the rest of my life. Miss Tidwell planted seeds of love and respect in my heart for all people, no matter where they come from or what they look like.

I learned an important lesson early on: don't judge people by what's on the outside. Instead, look beyond the surface into their spirit and soul. That's where real greatness lives.

I'm grateful to Miss Tidwell for being such a powerful example in my third year of school. I'll never forget her. She taught me not to judge, because you never truly know what kind of greatness someone carries inside.

I don't see color the way most people do. I don't focus on the outside; I feel the person, what makes them whole and complete. That's part of the vision you cast for yourself — to see beyond what's visible and find the true essence. If you can do that, if you can see and feel people that way, you become whole.

It's like the Holy Spirit, the soul inside each of us. That part needs to be fed, nurtured, and honored. You can't measure it by skin color or race. It just doesn't work that way. The real measure is the spirit, the heart, and the greatness waiting to be unleashed.

Reflection Prompt

- When was the last time you saw beyond the surface and connected with someone's soul?
- How can you guard your heart against judgment and cultivate compassion instead?

- What seeds of greatness have been planted in your life by unexpected people?

Prayer

Lord, help me to see beyond the outside of people. Help me to see only their soul. The part that You created and love. Teach me to embrace others with kindness and to reject judgment. May I nourish my own spirit with Your truth and walk the path of unity and love.

In Jesus' name, Amen.

Pause and Ponder this Scripture – Unity

Love one another deeply, from the heart. — 1 Peter 1:22

CHAPTER 12

The Power of Pickleball

Unless the Lord builds the house, the builders labor in vain. — Psalm 127:1

I didn't plan to build a pickleball court.

One day, I was just staring at this extra lot behind the house, thinking about mowing it every week, throwing money into the sprinkler system, and watching the water bill climb higher and higher. I thought, *This is ridiculous.* I'm sweating, I'm paying for it, and for what? Green grass, I don't even use.

So I poured a 30-by-50 concrete pad and turned it into a pickleball court.

Just like that, the yard had a new identity. The moment the court was done, everything shifted. Kids, neighbors, and adults all started showing up with a glint in their eyes, saying: "Byron, can we play?"

Of course, I answered, "Of course."

There are 20 houses in this neighborhood . I didn't invite anybody, but they came. They laughed. They battled. Some cried when they lost. I told them: "Get over it, come on, let's go again. We're not done."

That court became the pulse of the block.

It reminded me: you don't need a pulpit to lead. Sometimes, your backyard is your ministry. Sometimes, concrete and a net are enough to bring people together and remind them what joy feels like.

I built the court out of frustration. The grass was costing me more than it was worth, so I used what I had and turned a burden into a blessing. That's always been my way: take what's in front of you, shape it with intention, and let it become something meaningful. What started as a way to save time and money became a space for community, laughter, and connection. Funny how the things we build out of desperation can become the very things that bring us joy.

That sore spot in my yard became a soothing balm. It turned out that my pickleball court wasn't just a solution; it was a place where friendships could grow, where generations could play side by side, and where laughter could echo louder than complaints. What started as a fix became a foundation for fun. And I sure enjoy watching it bounce back.

Reflection Prompt

- What have you built — not just with your hands, but with your heart — that reflects who you are?
- How could something simple in your life become something meaningful for others?

Prayer

God, thank You for creativity, for vision, and for the little ideas that become big blessings. Show me how to keep building — not just spaces, but relationships, moments, and memories. Help me to serve joyfully and lead with love.

In Jesus' name, Amen.

Pause and Ponder this Scripture – Purposeful Building

Commit to the Lord whatever you do, and He will establish your plans. — Proverbs 16:3

CHAPTER 13

There's a Brighter Day Ahead

Weeping may endure for a night, but joy comes in the morning. — Psalm 30:5

One of the things I've come to value most in life is the steady light of my parents shining from the very beginning. I am not just sharing a memory here, but honoring the foundation they laid for me. From day one, they were special. And I believe every young person should be able to say that about their mom and dad.

We don't get to choose our parents. That decision was out of our hands. But the life we build from that starting point — that's something we do get to shape. Regardless of what kind of beginning you had, you have the power to build a future full of purpose, faith, and possibility.

My mother used to say something that stuck with me ever since I was a child: **"There's a brighter day ahead."**

Simple. Powerful. Prophetic.

When I heard her say it, I believed it. Not because the world was always bright, but because her voice carried hope. And now, as an adult, I've realized how much that phrase shaped my outlook. It became a platform I could stand on. A launching pad for faith. A reminder that no matter how dark the day seemed, the light was still coming.

That phrase still rings in my heart: **"There's a brighter day ahead."**

It helps me push through. It keeps me steady. It gives me the strength to dream big and speak life over my situation.

Maybe today you need that reminder too. That no matter what life looks like right now, joy is still on the horizon. Healing is possible. Restoration is within reach. And yes — there's a brighter day ahead.

Reflection Prompt

- Who in your life has spoken hope into you?
- What phrases or truths have stuck with you through hard seasons?
- Are you choosing to build your future with hope as the foundation?

Prayer

God, thank You for the people who have poured into me with love, truth, and hope. Thank You for the promises that remind me brighter days are ahead. Help me to carry those words with courage and pass them on to others. Even in the darkest moments, remind me that You're not finished and that Your light will shine again.

In Jesus' name, Amen.

Pause and Ponder this Scripture – Hope for the Future

"For I know the plans I have for you," declares the Lord, *"plans to prosper you and not to harm you, plans to give you a future and a hope."* — Jeremiah 29:11

3RD QUARTER

Rise and Respond

This is where the game can turn.

In the second half, a team shows what it's really made of. Are you coasting — or committing? The third quarter is about **ownership.** It's about leading your family, speaking truth, and rising when it's easier to stay down. This is where your faith stops being private and starts impacting the people around you. It's not about hype anymore — it's about heart.

1st Corinthians 16:13 says,

Be on your guard; stand firm in the faith; be courageous; be strong.

Now's not the time to play soft. Stand firm. Speak up. Live boldly. This is your moment to lead with strength and courage.

Call to Action

Step up for someone this month. Reach out to a brother, a son, or a teammate who needs encouragement, truth, or support. Leadership isn't about spotlight moments — it's about showing up consistently. Rise and respond — someone's waiting on you.

CHAPTER 14

She Gave Me Her Last Dime

She opens her mouth with wisdom, and the teaching of kindness is on her tongue... Her children rise up and call her blessed; her husband also, and he praises her.
— Proverbs 31:26, 28

You know, I watched my mother give when she had nothing left to give.

To me, my mother was a hero. The kind that never asked for anything in return. The kind who quietly handed you her last dime and went without so you didn't have to.

We were the kids eligible for free lunch. I never liked the idea of taking something I didn't earn. So my mother made sure I didn't feel less than. When she handed me her last $5 so I could get a hamburger at lunch like the other kids, it wasn't just about food — it was about dignity.

She sowed self-worth into my soul before I ever stepped on a football field.

And when the Green Bay Packers drafted me in 1983, I didn't think about buying a car or celebrating big. My first thought was of her. I'd made it to a place she only dreamed of, and I wasn't going to let her dreams go unnoticed.

So I handed her my checkbook.

It wasn't millions. But it was more than she or I ever dreamed. My signing bonus — $50,000. That checkbook to me was more than numbers. It was a message. A message I wanted to send to my mom, *I saw you go without. I never forgot. And now it's my turn to give.*

My mother never drove. Never had many needs. She was content with simple things.

And then there was my grandmother, Miss Willie Mae. She'd come to visit and spend the weekends. She never owned a color TV, never asked for much. But I remember the day I bought her a colored TV — something so ordinary by the world's standards, but her whole face lit up like it was Christmas morning.

She melted.

It reminded me that giving is about the heart behind it.

Looking back now, I'm grateful I didn't wait. My grandmother passed in February of 1988. My mother followed just months later in September, after a battle with cancer.

They were both gone in the same year. But not before they witnessed the wonderful and exciting life they helped build for me.

Their legacy wasn't money. It was love. It was selflessness. It was the power of sacrifice quietly shaping a son's future.

Reflection Prompt

- Who has made quiet sacrifices for you, ones you may not have fully appreciated at the time?
- What can you do now to honor their love, even if it's long overdue?

Prayer

Lord, help me to remember the ones who loved me when they had little to give. Remind me not to wait — to honor them with my words, my actions, and my life. Thank You for mothers and grandmothers who build empires out of pennies and prayers. May I live in a way that makes their sacrifices count.

In Jesus' name. Amen.

Closing Scripture

Honor your father and your mother, that your days may be long in the land that the Lord your God is giving you.
— Exodus 20:12

Byron's Mother Mrs. Lorene Williams

CHAPTER 15

The Power of Testimony

They triumphed over him by the blood of the Lamb and by the word of their testimony... — Revelation 12:11

Everybody's got a story — but our stories are not just for us. Our testimonies are what help others heal, grow, and believe.

I hope to help you understand that your story — your testimony, can help the next person. Every person you meet is a connection waiting to happen, a chance to impact someone's life.

I've got tons of stories. For example, when I run football camps, I choose the T-shirt colors based on the Super Bowl winner that year. For 2025, the shirts are green — the Eagles' color. For 2023 and 2024, they were yellow and red because of the Chiefs.

People ask me, "Why does that matter?" And I tell them — it's about connection and having a winning mindset. It's about relevance. Just think, every football player wants to be a part of a Super Bowl

Championship team. And it's about using what people recognize to open the door to something deeper.

We're all here on this Earth to help each other and navigate life's process, whatever your journey might be.

We grow from trials and tribulations. We overcome because of the hard stuff. Life experiences give us depth and perspective.

And here's what I want you to know more than anything else: You are not alone.

You may not believe but everybody is going through something at all times.

That's why your story — your testimony — is so important.

You may end up strengthening someone's soul because of it.

Reflection Prompt

- What part of your life story could serve as someone else's encouragement?
- Think of a trial you've overcome, and ask yourself how it might uplift someone else.
- Consider writing down your testimony or sharing it with a friend this week.

Prayer

Lord, thank You for the power of my testimony. Help me to recognize the value in my struggles and the purpose in my pain. Use my story to comfort and inspire others. Let my life be a light that leads people back to You.

In Jesus' name, Amen.

Pause and Ponder this Scripture — Comfort

He comforts us in all our troubles so that we can comfort others. When they are troubled, we will be able to give them the same comfort God has given us.
— 2 Corinthians 1:4

CHAPTER 16

The Power of the Process

Being confident of this, that He who began a good work in you will carry it on to completion until the day of Christ Jesus. — Philippians 1:6

I am always amazed at the perfect people God puts into our lives for every kind of purpose. Some to help us learn lessons, others so that we may help them learn lessons. Everything, everyone, and every moment has a purpose. Many times, the people or the circumstances were bridges that held us up when we didn't even know we were crossing over into something dangerous. God always fills the gaps.

When I go into schools and ask kids what they want to be, the majority of them don't know. That breaks me. Because if you don't know who you are or where you're headed, you're at risk. At risk of being misled. At risk of giving up. At risk of letting the world decide for you.

That's why I believe in tools like this journal. Something to hold, to write in, to reflect with. Something that says, "You're not alone, and your life can change." A playbook for your purpose in life. A remedy for confusion. A roadmap for rising up.

When you begin to discover who you are and why you're here, you don't just change *your* story — you set a new mark for your family. You shift the legacy. You redefine what's possible.

But it doesn't come easily.

The process matters.

We don't like to talk about it, but growth hurts. Trials test us. Pain shapes us. And even though we'd rather skip those chapters, they're essential to becoming whole. Every problem, every person placed in your life — God uses it. For your development. For your destiny.

This world doesn't just need more talent — it needs more people who are *motivated and dedicated.*

I have always asked our football campers:

- "Are you *Motivated*?"
- "Are you *Dedicated*?"
- "Are you an *MD*?"

Of course, they all reply saying, "No, I'm not. Medical doctor?!"

But I'm not talking about medical doctors. I'm talking about being around people who are motivated and dedicated. People who are committed to the *calling* over the comfort.

If you're reading this, you have stuck with the program and you are in the middle of the process right now. Don't run from it. Embrace it. God's not finished yet. Keep moving forward.

Reflection Prompt

- What part of the process are you currently in — planting, pruning, growing, or harvesting?
- Are you seeing the pain or the purpose?
- How might your current challenges be equipping you for something greater?

Prayer

God, thank You for the process — even when it's hard. Thank You for the people You've placed in my life and the path You're leading me down. Help me to stay motivated and dedicated, not just to success, but to significance. Give me eyes to see purpose in my pain, and strength to keep moving forward. I trust that You're working all things together for my good and Your glory.

In Jesus' name, Amen.

Pause and Ponder this Scripture – Perseverance

Let perseverance finish its work so that you may be mature and complete, not lacking anything. — James 1:4

CHAPTER 17

Love Everyone, But Don't Trust Everyone

But Jesus didn't trust them, because he knew all about people. No one needed to tell him about human nature, for he knew what was in each person's heart. — John 2:24–25

One of the greatest lessons I've learned is this: We are commanded to love everyone, but we are not required to trust everyone. That's not bitterness. That's the Bible. In the book of John, it tells us that even Jesus didn't entrust Himself to everyone, because He knew what was in people's hearts.

You can feel it when someone is trustworthy. And you can feel it when you need to be on alert, sensing that there is a bad sort of energy coming from someone. We all carry within us a special gift from God called intuition. It's a spiritual awareness that rises up inside you. I've experienced this many times in my life, and I'm sure if you're alert, you have too.

Years ago, I used to have this bad habit of letting my gas gauge get a little lower than I wanted it to go before fueling up again. One day, during my second year in the NFL, I was driving through Tennessee. My gas gauge showed it was past time for fueling up. I pulled into the nearest gas station, but something felt off. I looked around, some men were mingling there. A few of them stared at me like they had never seen a Black man before. It made me pause for a moment.

I heard the Holy Spirit whisper, *"Don't get out."*

I trusted that feeling. I decided not to get out of my car and fuel up, even though my gas gauge was showing empty. I drove ten more miles to a safer place. Yes, I was running low on gas, but I had to trust God more than the gauge.

That wasn't fear — that was discernment and the gift of intuition. And when I listened, that was spiritual obedience.

Discernment is a gift. Peter writes, "Stay alert! Watch out for your great enemy, the devil. He prowls around like a roaring lion, looking for someone to devour. Stand firm against him, and be strong in your faith" (1 Peter 5:8–9). We have to stay alert and listen so we can recognize danger.

You can love people without putting your life in their hands. Even the Bible distinguishes between love and trust. Love is a commandment. Trust is earned.

The enemy will try using people to distract or destroy you. That's why we must keep our spirits aligned with God's Word. Trust should be reserved for those who walk in integrity, who show you by their actions that they are safe to follow.

We are all vulnerable. Not everyone follows the path to Heaven. Not everyone will agree with you and how you're living your life. And we all have those moments when things aren't going exactly right. You must listen to your heart and stay alert.

Because here's the truth: If Satan can't destroy you, he will try to deceive you. And the enemy often uses people for the job. But God gives us the wisdom to know the difference. In the first book of Kings, chapter 19, we are told that Elijah didn't hear God in the wind or fire, but in the silence. Elijah heard God in a still, small voice. Like the whisper I heard, when the Holy Spirit said, "Don't get out." This voice that I am speaking of is not audible to anyone but you — because that voice is in your soul. It's meant for your ears only.

Reflection Prompt

- Can you think of a time when the Holy Spirit gave you discernment about a person or situation?
- What happened when you followed it?
- Is there someone in your life now you need to love from a distance?

Prayer

Lord, thank You for the wisdom of Your Word. Thank You for showing us how to love with grace but also with boundaries. Give me discernment in my relationships. Help me recognize when You are speaking to my spirit. And when I sense trouble, help me move wisely and without fear. Strengthen my faith and help me stay alert.

In Jesus' name, Amen.

Pause and Ponder this Scripture — Discernment

Dear friends, do not believe everyone who claims to speak by the Spirit. You must test them to see if the spirit they have comes from God. — 1 John 4:1

CHAPTER 18

The Spark of Encouragement

Therefore, encourage one another and build each other up, just as in fact you are doing. — 1 Thessalonians 5:11

Sometimes, it only takes one voice to change the entire direction of a life. For me, that voice came from two people: Miss Reed and Coach Reed.

Miss Reed was my fifth-grade teacher, and one of the first people outside my home who truly believed in me. My mom stayed at home and took care of everything, including people in our community, but Miss Reed gave me something else: vision.

She said something I'll never forget, "Byron, when you get to high school, I want you to meet Coach Reed."

I held on to that. I didn't know it then, but that seed she planted would grow into something powerful. Because when I got to ninth grade, I met Coach Reed, her husband. He became my track coach, and from day one, he challenged me in a way I'd never been challenged before.

"Byron," he said, "I'll make a deal with you."

"What kind of deal, Coach?"

"You make the A-B honor roll, and I'll give you $20 every six weeks."

That might not sound like a lot now, but back then? That was motivation. From ninth grade through twelfth, I sprinted to the gym every six weeks to collect that $20 bill. It wasn't just about the money — it was about the encouragement, the belief, the promise.

And you know what?

I graduated with a 3.8 GPA.

All because someone saw something in me and took the time to say, "You can do it." That's what encouragement does. It plants seeds. It starts fires. It builds futures.

Reflection Prompt

- Who encouraged you when you needed it most?
- What did they say or do that helped you push forward?
- This week, think about a young person in your life — or someone who may need a lift — and offer a word of genuine encouragement. It might change everything.

Prayer

Lord, thank You for the people You place in our lives to inspire and guide us. Help me to be that voice of encouragement for someone else. Use my words to uplift, my actions to support, and my heart to see the potential in others. Let me be the kind of person who helps others reach their full potential.

In Jesus' name, Amen.

Pause and Ponder this Scripture – Encouragement

Gracious words are a honeycomb, sweet to the soul and healing to the bones. — Proverbs 16:24

Mrs. Reed and Coach Reed

CHAPTER 19

Name the Football

Like newborn babies, crave pure spiritual milk, so that by it you may grow up in your salvation. — 1 Peter 2:2

There was a shift in my game — one that didn't come from training, coaches, or film study. This one came straight from God. I remember it clear as day: I was dropping too many passes. It wasn't about my hands — it was about my head. My focus was off. My heart wasn't locked in.

So I made a decision that changed everything. I gave the football a name: **Brandy**, after my oldest daughter. Every time that ball came toward me, I told myself, "Don't drop Brandy." After our second daughter was born, I renamed the football to **"Brand-Blair."**

That ball wasn't just leather and laces anymore. It was something precious. Something I couldn't afford to lose.

And when I made that shift — and started seeing that football as one of the most important things in my life — my drops disappeared.

I caught everything. Because I wasn't just catching a pass...I was holding onto something special.

That's what happens when you give what you're doing meaning. When you tie your effort to something greater than ego or applause. When your focus isn't just on making the team, but on not dropping the responsibility God placed in your hands.

Coach Tony Dungy once said, "The secret to success is good leadership, and good leadership is all about making the lives of your team members or family better." That starts with focus. With meaning. Choosing to see every responsibility you carry not as a burden, but as a blessing.

Don't drop what God placed in your hands. Call it by name. Carry it with care. Guard it like it's gold. Because someone else's future might be riding on your ability to stay locked in.

Modern neuroscience backs this up. Studies show that when we attach *personal significance* to an action — whether it's training, studying, or working — we increase both our motivation and retention. In other words, when your *why* is strong, your performance gets sharper. You're not just going through the motions.

You're locked in.

You're engaged.

Psychologists call it **"intrinsic motivation"** — doing something because it matters to you deeply, not because someone's watching. The minute I started calling the football "Brandy," my focus shifted from outcome to stewardship. I wasn't playing for stats. I was playing to honor something sacred. That level of intentionality is what separates good men from great ones.

Jesus said, *"Where your treasure is, there your heart will be also."* (Matthew 6:21). That means the things we guard, speak over, and treasure in our spirit become the things we give our best to. If your family matters to you, speak their names when you work. If your calling matters to you, treat it like your newborn baby. Speak over it. Focus on it. Carry it well.

Whether it's your role as a son, a father, a spouse, a mentor, a friend, or a follower of Christ — don't drop the ball. Name it. Guard it. Own it. Some things are too important to fumble.

Stop going through the motions. Stop letting distractions steal what matters most.

If someone you love is speaking, put down your phone and — LISTEN.

If you're working on something — FOCUS.

Motivational speaker Jim Rohn tells us, "When you work, work. When you play, play. Don't mix the two."

When you work, show up fully. Be disciplined. Eliminate distractions. Give it all you've got. Don't drift. Don't daydream. Get after it like it matters — because it does.

When you play — really play. Be present with your kids. Laugh hard. Rest well. Disconnect from the grind so you can refill your tank and return sharper.

The wisdom behind this is about mental clarity and balance. You're not torn between what you *should* be doing and what you *wish* you were doing. You're not cheating your work by thinking about leisure, and you're not cheating your rest by stressing over work.

It's about the integrity of effort. And for men who are building legacies, focus is your edge. When you work, work like a man on a mission. When you play, play like someone who knows how to celebrate God's goodness.

Use your superpower of undivided focus. When you're on the job, give it your all — no mental drift, no half-hearted effort. And when it's time to rest or enjoy life, be fully present in that too — don't let your mind be stuck on unfinished work. It's about honoring the moment you're in and dedicating your best to it.

God didn't call you to live scattered — He called you to live centered, grounded, and clear on your mission.

When you lock in on what He's put in your hands — your calling, your character, your kids — you become dangerous to the enemy and dependable to the people who count on you.

Your family doesn't need a man who's everywhere at once — they need a man who's present, prayerful, and fully engaged. Excellence in your calling will spill over into excellence in your home. And when your priorities are aligned, you'll start catching more than footballs — you'll start catching moments that matter for eternity.

Reflection Prompt

- What "football" are you holding right now in life — what has God entrusted to you that you need to protect and carry with focus?
- Is there a name you could give it to remind yourself that it matters?
- Where do you need to sharpen your focus and stop dropping what's been placed in your hands?

Prayer

Lord, thank You for trusting me with people, opportunities, and responsibilities that matter. Help me take them seriously. Help me to focus — not just for performance, but out of love and obedience. I don't want to drop what You've placed in my life. Strengthen my hands and sharpen my heart. Let me carry what You've given me with confidence, humility, and grace.

In Jesus' name, Amen.

Pause and Ponder this Scripture – Holding What Matters

Now it is required that those who have been given a trust must prove faithful. — 1 Corinthians 4:2

Byron Williams in Action

CHAPTER 20

Iron Sharpens Iron

As iron sharpens iron, so one person sharpens another.
— Proverbs 27:17

When I stood on stage at a fatherhood prayer breakfast, a phrase kept echoing: *"I need to be sharp."* And instantly, Proverbs 27:17 came to mind: *As iron sharpens iron, so one person sharpens another.*

But have you ever stopped to think about what it *really* takes to sharpen iron?

Sharpening iron isn't a delicate thing — it's intense and fierce. It's two hard materials coming together with force and friction. It's heat, sparks, and resistance. The blade doesn't get sharpened by brushing up against something soft. Wood doesn't sharpen iron. Foam doesn't sharpen iron. Even stone — if it's too brittle — won't do the job. You need something of equal strength. Something forged under pressure. Something that's been through the fire, too.

Why do we sharpen iron in the first place? Because dull blades are dangerous. A dull blade doesn't just make the work harder — it makes it riskier. You have to press harder and angle differently, but in doing so, you increase the chances of slipping and making a costly mistake. Ironically, a dull blade can cut you more easily than a sharp one, because it's unpredictable. You can nick yourself and others much more easily when you're working with something that isn't in its best condition.

Abraham Lincoln said, "Give me six hours to chop down a tree, and I will spend the first four sharpening the axe."

The same is true for men.

If you're called to lead — whether that's in your home, your community, your profession, or your ministry — you can't afford to be dull. You need clarity. Discernment. Strength. Wisdom. And that doesn't just happen on your own. It happens through contact. Through accountability. Through brotherhood.

Iron sharpens iron. Man sharpens man.

And just like with the blade, the sharpening process isn't always comfortable. It might feel like correction. It might come as tough love. It might look like a brother checking your blind spot, holding you accountable when you're slipping, or calling you higher when you'd rather coast.

But if it makes you better — it's worth it.

Ecclesiastes 4:9-10 tells us, Two are better than one, because they have a good return for their labor: if either of them falls down, one can help the other up. God didn't design us to be isolated. Lone wolves don't last long. We were created for connection. And in that connection, God builds strength. He raises up leaders who are humble enough to be sharpened — and strong enough to sharpen others. Brotherhood matters.

If you're serious about becoming the man God called you to be, are you positioning yourself with men who will sharpen you? Or have you and the men around you grown too soft to sharpen one another — and now you're just coasting? Look around, is anyone challenging you? Are *you* showing up to help sharpen others?

Because iron doesn't sharpen itself.

Reflection Prompt

- Do you have men in your life who challenge you, stretch you, and strengthen you?
- Are you willing to lean into that friction for the sake of growth?
- And are *you* a source of sharpening for someone else?

Prayer

Father, thank You for Your design — that we don't walk this path alone. Bring people into my life who will sharpen me with wisdom, truth, and love. Help me receive correction with humility and offer it with grace. Make me useful for Your purpose. Sharpen me daily, and let me sharpen others in return.

In Jesus' name, Amen.

Pause and Ponder this Scripture – Brotherhood & Accountability

Let us consider how we may spur one another on toward love and good deeds. — Hebrews 10:24

4TH QUARTER

Finish Strong

Legacies aren't built in the first quarter — they're sealed in the fourth.

Everything comes down to how you finish. Pressure's up. The clock's winding down. And in this moment, you've got to know who you are and whose you are. This section challenges you to leave it all on the field — spiritually, emotionally, and mentally. It's time to finish strong. Not for the crowd. Not for applause. But for the One who called you into the game in the first place.

In 2nd Timothy, we read,

I have fought the good fight, I have finished the race, I have kept the faith.

It's not about how you started — it's about how you finish. And finishing in faith is what matters most.

Call to Action

Think about how you want to finish this season. What's one thing you've started that needs closure? Make the call. Say the prayer. Do the hard thing. Don't just start well — decide right now to finish in faith and obedience.

CHAPTER 21

It's a Game of Inches

Be very careful, then, how you live — not as unwise but as wise, making the most of every opportunity…
— Ephesians 5:15–16

There's a reason they say football is a game of inches — because it is.

But you know what?

Life is too.

On the field, the difference between a win and a loss might come down to whether a toe stayed in bounds. One foot — one inch — can change the outcome of an entire game. Sometimes, it's not about speed, strength, or strategy. Sometimes, it's about awareness. Did the receiver drag his foot? Did the returning man step out? Did the lineman move too soon? It's those small margins — those near-miss moments — that make or break legacies.

When I say it's a game of inches, I mean it literally. You can run a 4.5 in the 40-yard dash and think you're blazing fast. But there's another

IT'S A GAME OF INCHES

guy running a 4.3 — just 12 inches behind you — and that split-second could be the difference between making a roster or missing it.

It's tight.

It's intense.

It's close.

But this principle goes far beyond football.

I think about races at the Olympics — high-stakes events where athletes train for years, even decades, for one shot. And sometimes, all that effort comes down to a single inch or less. In the 2008 Beijing Olympics, American runner Wallace Spearmon was a favorite in the 200-meter race. He crossed the finish line in third place, thinking he won the bronze medal, until officials disqualified him for stepping on the inside lane line. Not the whole foot — just the edge of his shoe grazed it.

An inch — or even less — cost him a medal and the dream of a lifetime.

That's how serious this is.

I've played with a lot of guys over the years. I've seen talent that could drop jaws — guys who could run faster, jump higher, and lift more than anyone else in the room. But you know what kept some of them from making it? It wasn't their skill — it was the mental side. They couldn't learn the plays. They wouldn't study the film. They didn't prepare when no one was watching.

Talent opens doors. Consistency keeps you in the room.

The inches matter.

Some men get passed over because they were too proud to learn. Others miss out because they were too distracted to notice the details. Don't be that man. Don't get disqualified over something that could've been corrected with humility.

This game of Life isn't much different than playing sports.

We don't always lose ground because of some big blowout mistake. A lot of times, we lose it inch by inch — by not paying attention. By living casually instead of intentionally. By thinking we've got more room than we actually do.

That's what Paul was getting at in Ephesians 5:15 when he said, "Be very careful, then, how you live — not as unwise but as wise." That's Bible talk for: "Watch your feet. Stay in bounds."

You may not be playing on the field, but you've still got sidelines to watch. There are boundaries in marriage, in money, in how you handle stress, how you talk to your kids, and what you let into your mind. One inch outside of God's design — and you can find yourself in a place you never meant to be.

Here's the hard part: it's not always obvious when you're stepping out. Most players don't mean to fumble. They're trying to score. But pressure hits, the ball slips, and now the whole game changes. And in life, a moment of carelessness can have a lasting impact.

- One text you shouldn't have sent.
- One conversation you didn't have.
- One decision you thought didn't matter.

You weren't trying to mess things up — but it happened all the same, because you weren't guarding the line.

The inches really do matter.

It's about awareness. The older I get, the more I understand that success doesn't always go to the strongest. It often goes to the man who pays attention. Who knows the rules. Who studies the film. Who keeps his eyes open when others are asleep.

IT'S A GAME OF INCHES

Football taught me that lesson over and over.

Sometimes, a guy gets X'd out of the equation — not because he didn't have talent, but because he didn't bring the whole package. In football, it's not enough to just be fast or strong. You've got to know the playbook, follow through on every rep, and show up mentally sharp. That's why it's so important to know your weaknesses — and just as important to know your strengths.

You've got to be honest with yourself. What are you good at? Where do you need to grow? Because the margin is tight, and the guys who make it — on the field or in life — are the ones who take their raw potential and do the work to turn it into real, measurable performance. They close the gap between who they are and who they're capable of becoming. And sometimes that is determined by only a little extra dedication and awareness.

God has given you talent, and he's also given you instruction. He's shown you where the boundaries are. Are you listening?

Because the enemy is watching those sidelines too — hoping you'll step just far enough out that he can call you out of the game.

And it's a game of inches…

Reflection Prompt

- Where in your life are you cutting it too close to the line?
- Are you living with wisdom, or just coasting on talent and not making the small details of life important?
- What does your awareness look like in your current season?

Prayer

God, help me pay attention. Not just in my day-to-day performance, but to my life position. Teach me to watch the boundaries You've set — not out of fear, but out of love and respect for the life You've called me to. Help me walk in wisdom, so that I may live with precision, and not waste the opportunities You send my way. Keep me from carelessness, and guide my steps every day, inch by inch.

In Jesus' name, Amen.

Pause and Ponder this Scripture – Inch by Inch

The prudent see danger and take refuge, but the simple keep going and pay the penalty. — Proverbs 22:3

CHAPTER 22

Discover What's Special

In His grace, God has given us different gifts for doing certain things well. — Romans 12:6

That verse is a reminder that no one else is wired exactly like you. There's something God put in you that He didn't give anyone else. And if you don't use it, the world misses out.

Maybe you used to paint. Or write. Or solve problems others couldn't. Maybe you were the one who made people laugh, or helped friends feel seen, or came up with solutions on the fly. Those are gifts — and gifts grow when we recognize them and steward them well.

We lose so much of that fire over time, especially when comparison creeps in or life tells us we're just "average." But nothing about God is average. And nothing He creates is common. Psalm 139:14 reminds us, *I praise you because I am fearfully and wonderfully made.* There's power in rediscovering what makes you light up. That's where your purpose often lives.

If you are around children ages two through five, never take them for granted; this is a powerful time in their lives. A fascinating study on divergent thinking revealed something profound: **98% of children ages three to five scored in the "genius" range** when asked to solve problems creatively. But by the time they reached ages eight to ten, that number dropped to 32%. By adolescence, it fell to 10%. And among adults over 25, only 2% still thought at a genius level.

This is a sad truth, and should be a wake-up call for every modern adult. It tells us that we are *born* creative. We're born full of imagination, innovation, and problem-solving power. But somewhere along the way, life starts teaching us to *color inside the lines*. School systems often reward memorization over innovation. Society pushes us toward sameness, toward fitting in, toward doing what's expected instead of dreaming what's possible. And over time, our creativity is not sharpened — it's suppressed.

That's not just a statistic — it's a warning shot. When we're young, we're not afraid to dream. Kids don't just *think* about the game — they *see* themselves in it. Ask a five-year-old, and they'll tell you they're going to play in the NFL, dunk like LeBron, or run in the Olympics. No fear. No filters. No limitations. Just passion, boldness, and imagination. They play without worrying if they'll be good enough. They celebrate their strengths before the world tells them to tone it down.

We love it when little kids tell us they want to be superheroes. We cheer them on when they say they'll fly to the moon or catch touchdowns in the Super Bowl. They create freely — because they haven't yet learned to be afraid of getting it wrong. Their imaginations make us smile. We celebrate their boldness.

But somewhere around middle school or graduation, the rules change. If a teenager stands up and says, "I'm going to be the greatest of all time," we flinch. If a high school senior says, "I want to direct movies," or "I'm going to the league," we start offering them a backup plan. Suddenly, the dreams that once delighted us become "unrealistic."

Why? Because we've lost touch with our own dreams. We hesitate. We wait for approval. We edit our ideas before they even leave our mouths.

We don't mean to kill the dream — but we tame it. We encourage safety over purpose, comfort over calling. If we believe God has placed a unique gift inside each of us, why would we tell someone to tone it down? You don't have to understand someone's calling to support it. And you don't need the world to validate your dream to keep pursuing it. Faith works by vision, not public approval.

The Word of God doesn't operate in fear. 2 Timothy 1:7 says, "For God has not given us a spirit of fear, but of power and of love and of a sound mind."

As we get older, life starts drawing boundaries. We trade freedom for form, imagination for instruction. Somewhere between learning the rules and following the crowd, many people stop playing bold. They stop believing they're special.

Athletes know this truth well: if you stop believing in yourself and hesitate only for a second, you miss the shot. If you doubt yourself off the line, you lose the race. Creativity works the same way. The ones who keep dreaming — the ones who stay loose and trust the gift — those are the ones who rise above.

In sports, it's often the player who's willing to take the risky shot — the one everyone else doubts — who ends up changing the game. That kind of boldness doesn't come from hype. It comes from knowing who you are and who gave you the gift.

So, whether you're 5 or 95, it's time to reclaim your imagination. Your dream isn't crazy. It's *custom-made*. Your gifts were wired into you on purpose. Don't let fear, fatigue, or outside opinions steal what God has already declared over you.

Romans 12:6 reminds us, "We have different gifts, according to the grace given to each of us." Grace *given*. Not earned, not compared, not borrowed. *Given*. You were born to stand out, not blend in. And just like a coach hands out playbooks based on position, God has placed something inside of you that fits the exact game you're meant to play.

So here's the challenge: stop burying the gift. Stop editing the dream. Get back in the game with the confidence you had when you were five — before the scoreboard ever mattered.

You were made to be special.

What does this mean for your spiritual walk? It means that rediscovering your God-given gifts often requires *unlearning* some of the fear and limitations you picked up along the way. It means giving yourself permission to explore again. To make mistakes. To dream bigger. To see with fresh eyes. Because God didn't stop giving creative assignments when you turned 10. He's still calling you to do things no one else can do *exactly* like you.

You don't outgrow your gift. But you *can* bury it under self-doubt, busyness, or neglect — but it's still yours.

Some people wait for someone else to validate them before they move forward, but you don't need permission to walk in your God-given purpose. You already have it. You just need to tune back in to what made you come alive before the world told you to tone it down.

It isn't about being special to the world — it's about understanding you were already chosen by God. You don't have to earn that. You just have to respond to it.

So go back. Reconnect with your gift. Read to your children. Sing in your living room. Build something with your hands. Write it down. Pray about it. Practice it. Your gift may not show up on a stage — but it can still make waves in your family, your neighborhood, your church, and your world.

You weren't given your gift by accident. It's not random — it's intentional. God's grace is expressed through your unique abilities, passions, and perspectives. Whether your gift is creativity, leadership, teaching, encouragement, or craftsmanship, it's meant to bless others.

Pause and ask yourself: **Am I using my gift — or hiding it?** God doesn't expect you to do everything. But He does expect you to do something with excellence, humility, and purpose.

Reflection Prompts

- What dreams did you have as a child that you've since buried or dismissed?
- Who discouraged you — and who believed in you? How did each voice shape your path?
- What would it look like today to honor the gift God placed inside you, without apology?
- Are you encouraging the young people around you to dream big — or are you passing on your fears?
- What would it look like to commit just 15 minutes a day to sharpen one of your God-given talents?

Prayer

Lord, help me rediscover the wonder You placed inside me. You created me with purpose, gifted me with imagination, and filled me with potential. Forgive me for the times I've doubted my calling, silenced my dreams, or shrank back in fear. Reignite the fire to pursue what makes me come alive — not for my glory, but for Yours.

Give me courage to speak boldly, create freely, and live fully, knowing that You have already qualified me. Help me to nurture the dreams in others, especially the young ones, so I never become the voice that dims their light.

In Jesus' name, amen.

Pause and Ponder This Scripture – Gifted for a Purpose

Each of you should use whatever gift you have received to serve others, as faithful stewards of God's grace in its various forms. — 1 Peter 4:10

CHAPTER 23

Check the Film

Search me, O God, and know my heart; test me and know my anxious thoughts. See if there is any offensive way in me, and lead me in the way everlasting.
— Psalm 139:23–24

One of the reasons I love football so much is that it's a level playing field. Everyone plays by the same rules. The game doesn't care what your background is, where you came from, or what your last is. When that whistle blows, it comes down to preparation, performance, and perseverance. Execution matters. It reveals everything and shows clearly all your strengths and your weaknesses. The game always reveals the truth. If you're not in shape, your body will break down.

But, no matter how ready you are, you're not going to win every play — and that's part of the process.

But that's not the point.

CHECK THE FILM

The point is growth.

One of the greatest tools in football is the film. The next day, you go back and watch the tape. And that tape doesn't lie. It shows everything — your strengths, your mistakes, your habits, your hustle. The tape doesn't allow for excuses. You might find out you made six errors in a game while someone else made two. That's not judgment; that's accountability. It defines the level of your performance. It shows exactly where you messed up, where you hesitated — and also where you shined. It shows the intangibles: your grit, your leadership, your mindset under pressure. It's not just a review — it's a revelation.

Watching the film is humbling, but it's also powerful. It's a teaching moment. A moment that defines where you really are in the game. The film review holds you accountable. It checks you.

This is something we're missing all too often at home and life in general. We don't have enough built-in checks and clear boundaries to plainly review our performance, so that we can say, "Okay, here's what I need to do to improve." We need that kind of reflection. And we can have it.

No discipline seems pleasant at the time, but painful. Later on, however, it produces a harvest of righteousness and peace for those who have been trained by it.
— Hebrews 12:11

Just like in the game of football, God gives us rules and clear boundaries so we know exactly how to play the game of life. He gives us tools for accountability, too. Scripture guides and checks us on every page.

The Word of God convicts, it corrects, and it trains us in righteousness, just like a coach who's trying to help you reach your full potential.

For many young men, when they join a football team, it's the first time they've had evident rules and boundaries. It's the first time someone has given them structure. It creates a team environment, a sense of family, a leadership hierarchy through coaches, and a set of clear rules. But even more than that, it gives them the opportunity to develop character, discipline, and resilience. That kind of foundation doesn't just help you win games — it helps you become a man.

And that's one of the reasons why I love the Bible even more than football. Because it gives me something to follow when the game of life gets chaotic. The Word of God lays out the principles and guidelines for life.

The field of football, as well as the field of life, both come with setbacks, missed plays, and moments when you wish you could rewind the clock. But God doesn't waste any of it. Every play is part of your growth. Every review is a chance to get better. That's why I hold tight to my banner verse, Romans 8:31*b*: *If God is for us, who can be against us?* It helps me stay rooted in truth — the kind of truth that gives you confidence, no matter what field you're standing in.

Just like football, God also creates a level playing field. His judgment is fair and without bias. Romans 2:11 says, *For God shows no partiality.* That means your status, your past, your connections — none of it gives you an advantage. What matters is your heart, your discipline, your obedience, and your faith.

And just like in the game, the film doesn't lie, God always sees the real you. He sees your effort, your intention, and your growth. And when the pressure hits, He's not looking at how you started, He's watching how you finish. Your effort in life matters. Your discipline matters. But it's your willingness to learn from your mistakes and check the film that will separate you from the already good people and the truly great people.

Football taught me to accept the critique, to learn from mistakes, and to keep showing up. God teaches me the same thing — through His Word, through the Holy Spirit, and through life itself. There's always a next play. There's always a lesson. And when you review it with honesty and humility, you grow.

Reflection Prompt

- What's an area of your life where you need to "check the film"?
- What are the patterns that keep showing up — and how is God using them to grow you?
- Do you have a banner verse to remind you who you are and where you're headed?

Prayer

Lord, thank You for the lessons You teach me through life and through Your Word. Help me to stay accountable, humble, and willing to grow. Show me my blind spots with love and wisdom. Let me walk with clarity, not pride — and help me use my strengths to serve You and others.

In Jesus' name, Amen.

Pause and Ponder this Scripture – Honest Review

All Scripture is God-breathed and is useful for teaching, rebuking, correcting, and training in righteousness.
— 2 Timothy 3:16

CHAPTER 24

Are You Called to Go or Stay?

I will lead the blind by ways they have not known, along unfamiliar paths I will guide them; I will turn the darkness into light before them and make the rough places smooth. These are the things I will do; I will not forsake them.
— Isaiah 42:16

There comes a time in every man's life when he has to answer a hard question: Is it time to go, or time to stay? Am I meant to hold the line where I am — or is God calling me forward into something new?

That's not always an easy call. Especially when you've been building something for years. Ask any NFL player, and they'll tell you that you never really know when your last play is coming. One minute, you're suited up, fighting for yards. The next, it's over. Just like that.

For most players, the end isn't neat. It's not celebrated. It's painful. Some leave the game hurt. Others leave bitter. Many leave broken.

The stats don't lie. Divorce rates among NFL players are between 60 - 80%. And why? Because when you've given everything to something — when it's been your identity since you were ten years old — letting go can feel like death. But that's where the next question matters even more: Will you let God lead you into the next chapter?

Isaiah 42:16 isn't just a comfort — it's a call to trust. God says He will lead us through unfamiliar paths, and that He'll turn darkness into light. Even when we can't see the road, He knows the way.

That's exactly what happened to Jock McKissick. After being drafted by the Bengals, he had his future lined up. But because of an old injury, the dream was taken from him in an instant. No warning. No exit plan. One day he was part of the team; the next, he was just… done. He had no choice but to leave his dream of being a professional football player behind. It was time to go.

Like all football players who start a new chapter, years of structure, coaching, routine, and direction were gone. Jock had to learn how to live without someone telling him where to be, what time to show up, or how to prepare for game day. That's not just a shift — it's a redefining moment.

But listen: In Isaiah 30:21, God tells us, *"Whether you turn to the right or to the left, your ears will hear a voice behind you, saying, 'This is the way; walk in it.'"* When you belong to God, your calling doesn't end when one chapter closes. It just shifts.

The same God who called you to the field can call you to the next assignment. And sometimes, the greater mission starts *after* the stadium lights go out.

Because of Jock's spiritual foundation, after his impressive college football career ended — and his hopes of playing for the Bengals were shattered by injury — he didn't let that setback define him. Instead of staying stuck in disappointment, he leaned into a new calling, going on to become an actor, producer, and author, using his talents and platform to impact others. In his free time, he travels the country speaking with parents, teachers, and young people, urging them to live their best lives with purpose and intention.

In his book *50 Principles to Thrive in Life*, Jock gives great advice for the person wondering whether to stay or go, "Give yourself credit for all the ground that you've covered, all the things you've learned, all the things that you've accomplished up until this certain point. You've accomplished so much and gained so much more perspective."

You are more than your job, your title, your jersey, or your position. You are a man of God — and He will not forsake you. Deuteronomy 31:8 specifically states,

---

The Lord himself goes before you and will be with you; he will never leave you nor forsake you. Do not be afraid; do not be discouraged.

Now, maybe you're reading this and thinking, "Yeah, that's fine for guys with big titles and obvious talent. But you don't know my story. I don't have anything like that. I don't have a backup plan. I don't even know what I'm good at."

Let me stop you right there: Yes, you do. You may not see it yet, but God does. Remember earlier when we talked about your TAG — your Talents, Abilities, and Gifts? That wasn't just a motivational acronym. That is Truth. God created you with something inside that this world needs.

You don't need a platform to be valuable. You don't need a spotlight to shine. What you need is the faith to believe that what God placed in you is real, and the courage to start walking in it.

Ask Him to show you.

Then get up, and go be who He called you to be.

You might be standing at a crossroads right now. Should you move forward — or dig in and stay? Should you take that new job, step out in ministry, or finally let go of what used to define you?

Seek Him. He still speaks. And when He calls you, follow. Even if you feel blind — He will guide you.

Reflection Prompt

- Are you in a season of transition right now?
- What are you holding onto that God may be asking you to release?
- Where do you need to trust that He will lead you — even if you can't see the path?

Prayer

Lord, sometimes life brings uncertainty. Sometimes I don't know which way I'm being called, especially where I've planted roots and things change and shift. Help me to know whether You're calling me to go — to step out, to grow, to trust You in unfamiliar places or to dig in and stay the course. I don't want to move ahead of You, and I don't want to fall behind You. So I ask You, God, lead me.

If You're calling me to stay, then help me stay with strength. Help me stay present. Stay committed. Stay faithful. Help me not keep my eyes on the mission right where I am and not become busy by wishing I was somewhere else.

If You're calling me to go, give me courage. Make me bold enough to leave what's comfortable and step into the unknown. Help me trust that even when I can't see the road ahead, You've already gone before me. Close the doors that need to be closed. Open the ones only You can open. And give me peace, even before I see the outcome.

I want to move — or stay — in obedience. Because no matter where I am, or what I am doing, I want to be in the center of Your will.

In Jesus' name, Amen.

Pause and Ponder this Scripture – Trusting God's Lead

This is what the Lord says—your Redeemer, the Holy One of Israel: "I am the Lord your God, who teaches you what is good for you and leads you along the paths you should follow." — Isaiah 48:17

CHAPTER 25

The Inner Spirit

The light shines in the darkness, and the darkness has not overcome it. — John 1:5

What I've come to realize is that we all have something inside of us — a light that needs to shine. But the world is full of darkness, and that darkness has a way of stifling potential if you let it. I've seen it on every team, every city, every stop along my 12-year journey from Green Bay to Philly, New York to Canada, Detroit to the World League. And back again.

But when you know where your help comes from, you stop performing and start walking in purpose. That's when the shift happens. It's not about "what I'm doing" — it's about how others can see the way you're doing it. Because too many people are stuck in the dark. And that's not where we're meant to live.

God feeds our souls through light. That's where you get your strength. That's where your vision is born. That's where your real sprint comes from. A coach can teach you how to run a route, but he can't coach your speed. And he can't coach your inner sprint — that part of you that is inside. The part that gets you to your destination and helps you finish strong.

In my senior year of college, I only caught 26 passes. But eight of those were touchdowns, and over 500 yards came from those few catches. Why? Because of the speed, the inner spirit, that separated me. And that's what separates all of us.

There's a growing body of research showing that athletes who are grounded spiritually tend to outperform expectations, not just in terms of physical ability, but in emotional resilience and mental clarity. Studies from institutions like the University of Florida and Baylor University show that athletes with a strong faith foundation are more likely to cope well with stress, maintain focus under pressure, and persevere through injuries and uncertainty. Faith becomes their anchor. It gives them something deeper than the spotlight or the scoreboard. They're not just playing for applause — they're playing with purpose. They run with conviction because they know they're part of something eternal.

When your spirit is aligned with something greater than yourself, the pressure lifts. You're no longer defined by the outcome of a game or the highs and lows of performance. Your identity is rooted in the One who gave you the gift in the first place. That's the inner spirit people talk about but can't always explain — the quiet strength that rises up when your body's tired, when the odds are stacked against you, when no one else believes.

The inner spirit is the real fuel. It's that quiet fire that says, *"There's more in you."* It keeps you running when your legs are tired. It keeps you hopeful when the doors close. And when you know who you are in God, when you really know, you don't just run harder.

You run freer.

Reflection Prompt

- Where is God developing your "inner spirit "?
- Think of a time when someone saw the light in you — even if you didn't see it yourself.
- How can you be that light for someone else?

Prayer

God, remind me that the real strength I need doesn't come from talent or appearance — it comes from You. Feed my soul with Your light, and help me be a light for someone walking in the dark.

In Jesus' name, Amen.

Pause and Ponder this Scripture – Strength

But those who hope in the Lord will renew their strength. They will soar on wings like eagles; they will run and not grow weary, they will walk and not be faint. — Isaiah 40:31

CHAPTER 26

Finishing Strong

His divine power has given us everything we need for a godly life through our knowledge of him who called us by his own glory and goodness. — 2 Peter 1:3

I've seen it too many times to count — men and women who started strong, had big dreams, even reached the mountaintop… but didn't finish well. Maybe it was a scandal. Maybe they got worn out, gave up, or gave in. Either way, it hurts to watch. Especially when you know the potential they once had.

The truth is, there are forces working against us every single day:

- the world
- the flesh
- the devil

And they don't sleep.

- The world tries to mold us into something we're not. It pressures us to conform, telling us who we should be, what we should chase, and what should matter most.
- The flesh is tricky. It tempts us to take shortcuts, to please ourselves, to quit when things get uncomfortable.
- And the devil? He'll use every subtle, slick trick in the book to get us off track. He won't just attack your weakness — he'll wait till you're strong, confident, and successful… and then hit you where you least expect.

But here's the hope: God has already equipped us. 2 Peter reminds us that His divine power has given us everything we need to live a godly life. That means we don't fight empty-handed. We fight with faith, with wisdom, with His Word. We fight with prayer, accountability, and humility. That's how you finish strong.

Sometimes God doesn't test you when you're at your lowest. He tests you when you're at your highest. When the money's right. When the attention is flowing. When the spotlight's on. That's when He watches to see — will you still walk with Me? Will you still trust Me? Will you still honor Me?

I want my life to say yes. I want to be known not just for how I started, but how I finished. Because finishing strong isn't just about winning. Finishing strong is about being faithful to the end.

Watch my 2-minute warning video on YouTube here: https://youtu.be/lmTYcZ5HAs4

In football, the two-minute warning doesn't always mean it's the end of the game, but it does mean it's time for the players to shift. The pressure turns up. The decisions matter more. The game is still going, but now every second counts. That's when champions focus. That's when leaders lead. And most importantly, that's when you decide now is the time to finish strong.

Life comes at us with its own two-minute warnings — not just at the end, but throughout your journey. You might be in high school trying to stay focused. You might be navigating manhood, family, failure, or a dream that feels too far. Whatever phase you're in, the two-minute warning is that moment where God says: *"Now it's time. Move like it matters."*

Below is a link to a short 2-minute video that shows some of my NFL highlights. But it's bigger than football. It's a reminder that every phase of your life will come with pressure, purpose, and a clock you don't control.

That's what James 4:14 is really about: Why, you do not even know what will happen tomorrow. What is your life? You are a mist that appears for a little while and then vanishes.

That's Bible talk for: Life is short. Unpredictable. Fragile. So don't waste it. Don't wait. Live with purpose, not procrastination.

You don't always get a second half. You won't always get overtime. So when your two-minute moment shows up, *be ready*.

Focus. Lock in. Lead.

☞ Watch My 2-Minute NFL Highlights – https://youtu.be/lmTYcZ5HAs4

You've been drafted for greatness. The clock is ticking. Finish strong. Play like it matters… because it does.

Reflection Prompt

- Are you relying on your own strength or on God's power to finish strong?

- Which of the three forces — the world, the flesh, or the devil — seems to be pressing on you most right now?
- What habits or relationships are helping (or hurting) your ability to endure?

Prayer

God, thank You for giving me everything I need to live a godly life. Help me to recognize the pressures that try to pull me away from You — whether it's the world's influence, the weakness of my flesh, or the enemy's lies. Strengthen me for the long haul. Give me the desire and discipline to stay faithful. And when I'm tested, remind me of who I am in You, and who You've called me to be.

In Jesus' name, Amen.

Pause and Ponder this Scripture – Finishing Strong

> *His divine power has given us everything we need for a godly life through our knowledge of Him who called us by His own glory and goodness. Through these, He has given us His very great and precious promises, so that through them you may participate in the divine nature, having escaped the corruption in the world caused by evil desires. For this very reason, make every effort to add to your faith goodness; and to goodness, knowledge...* — 2 Peter 1:3–5

OVERTIME

When It's Not Over Yet

Sometimes the game goes longer than expected. So does the fight.

Overtime is unfamiliar territory. It's where the clock doesn't matter — only the heart does. Spiritually, overtime represents seasons of waiting, uncertainty, or spiritual battle. When you thought God would have answered by now. When you're tired, but you still have to show up. This section is for the moments when you want to give up but grace pulls you forward.

You need to persevere so that when you have done the will of God, you will receive what He has promised.
— Hebrews 10:36

There's a reason you're still standing. And there's a reward if you keep going. When the battle drags on, God brings renewal. You may be tired, but He is not done.

Call to Action

Don't tap out. Take five quiet minutes today to ask God for renewed strength. Write down one promise from His Word that you'll hold onto during this section — and declare it every time you feel tired or discouraged. Overtime isn't over — God's still moving.

CHAPTER 27
Fifty Plus One

But those who hope in the Lord will renew their strength. They will soar on wings like eagles; they will run and not grow weary, they will walk and not be faint. — Isaiah 40:31

We all have turning points — moments when we either press forward or fall back. For me, one of those moments came in high school. It started with a mistake and ended with a lesson that would follow me for the rest of my life.

I was a senior, running track to stay in shape for football season. But one day, some of my teammates and I got caught drinking at a track meet. I was never one to lie about anything, so I came clean with the coach who was interrogating us.

The coach said, "Byron, I really want to tell you how much I appreciate you, because you told the truth. I know some of the other guys didn't."

I was touched by the heartfelt love I was feeling from him. I was upset with myself and the mistake I had made. It was an emotional moment I was tearing up, and so was my coach.

I'll never forget when he looked me in the eyes, put his hand on my shoulder, and said, "You're better than that. I know what a great guy you are."

My coach could have kicked me off the team, but, instead, he gave me a choice: run 50 miles (every mile in under eight minutes) if I wanted to play football.

I agreed.

I thought I could handle it. Five miles a day for two weeks sounded hard but doable. I ran Monday through Friday and racked up 25 miles that first week. I was proud of that. Then came the second Monday. I hit my 28th mile. That's when my coach pulled me aside and said, "Byron, you didn't make your miles."

What?

I was stunned. I thought I was on pace. But he just shook his head. "You didn't make your miles."

So I ran more. I pushed myself harder than I ever had. And something happened on one of those extra miles — mile 51. I was out there, legs aching, lungs burning, and that's when God spoke to me.

He said, "You're going to play pro football for 12 years."

I didn't hear it out loud, but I felt it deep in my spirit. It was one of those moments when you know that you know.

On the final Friday of that second week, I crossed the finish line on my 51st mile. I called it "Fifty Plus One." I ran what was required — and then some.

Two weeks later, my coach came up to me. He said, "Byron, you know you made your miles the first week, right?"

I blinked. "What?"

He nodded. "I just wanted to see if you were going to quit."

I didn't quit.

I tell this story because "ain't nobody perfect." You will make mistakes in life, but always be true to yourself and others to give yourself the best chance. And a chance to make it right.

That was 1979. Fast forward 30 years to 2009. My old high school called me up and asked if I could put in a proposal for a new track. *After football, I went into the track and turf business for 25 years.*

God literally gave me almost $1,000 for every mile I ran back then. I got paid $50,000 to help rebuild that same track. But that last mile — mile 51, for that I received something even greater — Wisdom, Discipline, Perseverance, and Commitment. I truly believe mile 51 gave me the stamina and confidence I needed to become a professional football player.

I think about those miles all the time. Not *just* the miles, but what they represented: grit, second chances, and God's favor. And how what felt like punishment became preparation.

Those steps I took back then? They were ordered by the Lord. Every single one. So, in 2011, my High School started honoring our HS athletes, so my HS mentor Willie Teal, former LSU defensive back for Minnesota Vikings, and I were the first two athletes to be in the inaugural class.

And now, 30 years after that long run, God gave me the opportunity to give back.

Reflection Prompt

- Can you recall a time in your life when you had to endure something hard, only to later see how God used it for your growth or blessing?
- What did you learn from that experience?
- This week, ask God to reveal the purpose in your current challenges — and to show you how your obedience now might bless others later.

Prayer

Lord, thank You for ordering my steps — even when they're difficult, even when I don't understand. Help me to trust Your plan and endure with faith. Use my past to bless others in the present. Let every mile, every mistake, and every miracle point back to You.

In Jesus' name, Amen.

Pause and Ponder this Scripture – Endurance

I have fought the good fight, I have finished the race, I have kept the faith. — 2 Timothy 4:7

CHAPTER 28

Moving Mountains

If you have faith as small as a mustard seed, you can say to this mountain, "Move from here to there," and it will move. Nothing will be impossible for you. — Matthew 17:20

Faith is not just something you carry — faith carries you. It picks you up when life drops you. It moves you when you feel stuck. It holds you steady when the ground under you shifts. NFL Quarterback, Russell Wilson, says, "My faith is the core of who I am. I give all glory to God. Without Him, I am nothing."

In my own life — after injuries, disappointments, or when I thought it was the end of my football career — I held on to what I had seen modeled. I remembered my parents' faith, and I chose to believe that God was still writing my story and that the doors I thought were closed were just being prepared to open.

I've learned over time that when your faith is your foundation and you are anchored in God, you can walk into situations that don't make sense and still feel peace. That's how I've lived much of my life — trusting in what I couldn't see yet, but knowing deep in my spirit that God was working it all together for good.

That's why I had the poster on my wall when I first got to UTA.

Trust in the Lord with all your heart and do not lean on your own understanding; in all your ways acknowledge Him, and He will direct your path. — Proverbs 3:5–6

That verse became my anchor. Every time I read it, I felt like God was reminding me: I got you. Stay faithful. Keep walking.

Faith gives you a kind of spiritual eyesight. It lets you see beyond the struggle to what God might be doing behind the scenes. You may not know how, or when, but you believe He's working — and that's enough.

Because here's the truth: life will challenge you, but faith will carry you through. And when you look back, you'll realize it wasn't luck. It wasn't a coincidence. It was faith that sustained you.

There are so many scriptures that tell us just how important having faith really is:

- Galatians 2:16 reminds us, *Know that a person is not justified by the works of the law, but by faith in Jesus Christ.*

- Hebrews 11:6 declares, *Without faith it is impossible to please God, for the one who draws near to Him must believe that He exists and that He rewards those who earnestly seek Him.*

- 2 Corinthians 5:7 is one of my favorites: *For we walk by faith, not by sight.*

- And in Mark 11:22–24, Jesus says, *"Have faith in God. Truly I tell you, if anyone says to this mountain, 'Be lifted up and thrown into the sea,' and does not doubt in their heart, but believes what they say will happen, it will be done for them. Therefore, I tell you, whatever you ask for in prayer, believe that you have received it, and it will be yours."*

When that moment comes — when your faith connects with God's will — you'll realize that the very forces of hell are powerless against you, and all the resources of heaven are backing you up.

Faith is often quiet. It doesn't always show up in miracles or big signs. Sometimes it shows up in the quiet "yes" of a parent who believes in you, or the courage to keep walking even when you can't see what's ahead.

Faith isn't just a belief — it's a lifeline. Countless studies show that faith and spirituality aren't only good for the soul — they're good for our bodies and minds, too.

Faith is more than a feeling; it offers real protection and healing. A global review of more than 498 studies found that higher religious involvement is associated with better mental health outcomes — less depression, fewer suicidal thoughts, less substance abuse, and overall greater life satisfaction.

Here are a few stats broken down:

- Meta-reviews of hundreds of studies consistently show that higher religious or spiritual involvement is linked to less anxiety and depression, improved psychological well-being after trauma, and greater overall life satisfaction and resilience.
- *The National Library of Medicine* found that adults with type-2 diabetes showed that stronger religious faith led to significantly

greater resilience, which then helped reduce stress and improve coping by over 61%.

- U.S. military veterans with high levels of faith and religious commitment had notably lower risks of PTSD (about 54% lower), major depression (50% lower), and alcohol use disorders (34% lower) compared to less religious peers.

Reflection Prompt

- When in your life have you had to walk by faith and not by sight?
- What legacy of faith were you handed by those who came before you?
- Is there someone in your life now who needs your encouragement — your belief — in them?

Prayer

Lord, thank You for the gift of faith passed down through generations. Thank You for the examples of those who trusted You when things didn't make sense. Help me to be that kind of person for others — to give, to believe, and to build even when I can't see the full picture. Lord, open my eyes, and don't stop working until I see what You want me to see. Strengthen my trust in Your plan, and help me to live a life that reflects Your faithfulness.

In Jesus' name, Amen.

Pause and Ponder this Scripture – Faith That Endures

We live by faith, not by sight. — 2 Corinthians 5:7

CHAPTER 29

Feeding the Wolves

Do not be overcome by evil but overcome evil with good.
— Romans 12:21

There's an important lesson that comes from an old Native American parable. It's about two wolves living inside every person — a story that teaches you about the battle within your own spirit.

There are two wolves inside of you. One is good, filled with kindness, hope, and love. It wants all the good things life can offer. The other wolf is the opposite — full of hate, anger, and negativity. It attacks, it takes, it destroys.

The question is: which wolf will win? The answer is simple but profound — the wolf you feed the most is the one that comes out.

It's why I stay away from negative people — those who complain constantly or bring bad energy wherever they go. I speak to everyone, but once I sense bad energy, I step back. I protect my space because I know what feeding the wrong wolf does.

You can feel it when someone walks into a room. If they are good or bad. If their energy is light, you feel good and want to be around that person. If they have heavy energy — you know something's off right away. I learned to trust that feeling.

When I was playing professional football, I remember walking into rooms where guys were doing drugs. I turned right around and walked out because I promised myself I wouldn't let that poison touch my life.

I lost too many people to those kinds of habits. I knew that if I gave in, even once, it could destroy me. I never even tried smoking a joint. I made a choice early on to feed the good wolf — to protect my spirit and my purpose.

I truly believe those kinds of bad habits hurt more than just the person using them. They make you lazy and shiftless. I don't know anyone who made it big by feeding the wrong wolf. None of the people I respect ever benefited from that life.

Being a leader here in Dallas, I've had to help a lot of guys find their way back from the darkness. It all comes back to giving more attention to what is good and pure in your life, and staying back and away from the things or people that will drag you down.

If you are near a person, place, or circumstance that could hold you back from your dreams, step back and think for a moment about the future you want, the people you love, and the things you want to accomplish in life before making a choice that could put an end to everything good in your life now, and in your future.

Reflection Prompt

- Think about what you've been feeding lately. What kinds of thoughts, habits, and people are you inviting into your life?

- How can you nurture the good so that your spirit grows stronger each day?

Prayer

Lord, help me to feed the good inside me — fill me with love, hope, and kindness. Guard my heart from darkness and negativity. Teach me to protect my spirit and to walk the path of righteousness and peace. May Your light guide me every day.

In Jesus' name, Amen.

Pause and Ponder this Scripture – Choosing Good

Finally, brothers and sisters, whatever is true, whatever is noble, whatever is right, whatever is pure, whatever is lovely, whatever is admirable — if anything is excellent or praiseworthy — think about such things. — Philippians 4:8

CHAPTER 30

The SWOT Team

For God gave us a spirit not of fear but of power and love and self-control. — 2 Timothy 1:7

We spend a lot of time looking outward — at what other people are doing, at what the world expects, at what the culture tells us we should be. But the most powerful growth doesn't happen when we look out. It happens when we look in. One of the most useful tools I've come across to help do that is something called the **SWOT** analysis. It stands for **Strengths, Weaknesses, Opportunities, and Threats**. When applied honestly, it can change your life.

Let's break it down:

S is for Strengths

These are the things that come naturally to you — your talents, your skills, your passions, the things that light you up when you do them. But don't just stop at identifying them. Strengths must be sharpened. A gift is only as good as what you do with it. Ask yourself: How am

I using what God gave me? Am I putting in the work to turn natural talent into excellence? Strengths are the foundation you build on, but a foundation only matters if you start building something on top of it.

W is for Weaknesses

This part takes honesty. What do you struggle with? Where do you fall short? Maybe it's procrastination, self-doubt, poor time management, or even fear. Weaknesses aren't something to be ashamed of — they're just areas that need your attention. Don't hide from them; address them. Invite mentors in. Seek accountability. Remember: God's power is made perfect in weakness (2 Corinthians 12:9). But first, you've got to name it before you can change it.

O is for Opportunities

Opportunities are the blessings you don't control, but you can prepare for them. A scholarship. A new connection. A job offer. A divine appointment. The world is full of doors, but they don't open forever. That's why you have to stay ready. Ask yourself: Am I in the right rooms? Am I showing up prepared? Am I speaking life or defeat when opportunity knocks? What you do in the dark will determine how bright your moment is when the spotlight hits.

T is for Threats

Threats are the things that come against you, internally or externally. It might be fear, temptation, negative influences, family dysfunction, peer pressure, or even social media. Threats are real, and they're coming whether you prepare or not. The key is knowing where you're vulnerable and staying rooted in God's truth. The enemy would love nothing more than to distract you, discourage you, or detour you from your purpose. But when you know your threats, you can set up guardrails. You can pray smarter, plan better, and resist harder.

Knowing who's on your SWOT team doesn't mean you'll never struggle. But it means your strategy won't be left to chance. You'll move with awareness. You'll live with intentionality. And that's the key to growth.

Reflection Prompt

- Take time to list your top three strengths and how you're using them.
- Name at least one weakness you're ready to work on.
- What opportunities are already around you that you may have been ignoring?
- Are there any threats you need to set boundaries around?

Prayer

Father, thank You for creating me with a purpose. Help me to embrace both my strengths and my struggles, knowing You can use them all. Open my eyes to the opportunities You're placing in front of me, and give me wisdom to protect myself from the threats that try to distract or destroy. Shape me into someone who doesn't just survive, but thrives — on purpose and with purpose.

In Jesus' name, Amen.

Pause and Ponder this Scripture – Self-Awareness

Examine yourselves to see whether you are in the faith; test yourselves. Do you not realize that Christ Jesus is in you — unless, of course, you fail the test? — 2 Corinthians 13:5

CHAPTER 31

A Super Bowl and a Super Moment

For I was hungry and you gave me food, I was thirsty and you gave me drink, I was a stranger and you welcomed me.
— Matthew 25:35

It was 2007, and a really cold day in Detroit, Michigan — the kind of chill that clings to your soul. If you've ever been to Detroit in the wintertime, you understand that the cold goes past your coat and gets under your skin. There was a reason that the Super Bowl was being held there on that icy day. You see, the NFL has what they call a golden rule: if a city builds a new stadium, they're promised the chance to host a Super Bowl within five years. So Detroit, though freezing in February, got its turn.

The city was buzzing with Super Bowl energy, but beneath the lights and celebration, something else stirred in me that day. I noticed a man outside a church's soup kitchen. He was hunched over, clearly homeless, shivering in the bitter air, with nothing.

I don't believe anything happens by accident. I couldn't just walk past this man. That day, I had bought some Super Bowl merchandise — souvenirs and memorabilia. I returned to my car, gathered what I had, and brought it to him — gifts, yes, but more importantly, I was encouraged by the Holy Spirit to share a word from the Lord. I gave him some money too, but what I really wanted to give him was hope.

I looked him in the eye and told him, "God is going to reveal to you one day why you're going through this. He hasn't forgotten you. You will see that even though you are homeless, He's walking you through the process right now."

Then I asked him a simple question: "When's your birthday?"

"February 23rd," he quickly replied, as he wondered why I cared.

That's when I encouraged him, "Go to the Bible and search the Word of God and find a verse with 23 in it. Read a verse, read a chapter, and find something that really speaks to you."

I didn't give him a specific verse — I told him to look in Matthew, maybe John, and just read until something deep within is sparked. Because I believe the Word is alive. I believe when you open your heart and your Bible at the same time, something sacred happens.

I don't know exactly what happened to that man after we parted ways. But I know what I *believe*: I believe he found his verse. I believe God met him right where he was. And I believe he's not homeless anymore because: *The Lord is near to the brokenhearted and saves the crushed in spirit.* — Psalm 34:18. Maybe not just in the physical sense, but in the spiritual sense too — because sometimes home is knowing who you are in Christ.

The Super Bowl may have brought thousands to the city that day. But God had His eye on just one man. And maybe He sent me there not for the game, but for a divine appointment.

> *Do not neglect to show hospitality to strangers, for thereby some have entertained angels unawares.* — Hebrews 13:2

This verse reminds us that when we follow God's lead — even when it feels small or unimportant — He is directing our path. Just like that day in Detroit, God may use *your* steps to change someone else's life. Let today be a reminder that your acts of kindness are seeds. You may not always see the fruit, but God does. And He honors every step you take toward loving your neighbor, especially the ones we tend to overlook.

Reflection Prompt

- Think back to a time when you helped someone in need — or wished you had.
- What kept you from acting, or what inspired you to move?
- This week, ask God to open your eyes to the people around you who may be cold, hungry, lonely, or spiritually homeless.
- How can you be part of their turning point?

Prayer

Lord, thank You for using ordinary moments for extraordinary purposes. Give me eyes to see those who need encouragement, and a heart ready to give without hesitation. Let me never overlook the one in front of me. Remind me that even a small act of kindness can be a turning point in someone's life.

In Jesus' name, Amen.

A SUPER BOWL AND A SUPER MOMENT

Pause and Ponder this Scripture –with 23

The steps of a good man are ordered by the Lord: and he delighteth in his way. — Psalm 37:23

SUPER BOWL

Victory in Christ

We don't fight for victory — we fight from it.

This is where glory meets gratitude. In football, the Super Bowl is about the ring, the prestige, and the glory. But this victory isn't about fame — it's about faithfulness. This section celebrates the wins, reflects on the journey, and honors the One who carried you through every quarter. You didn't make it here alone. God brought you. So now it's time to worship, reflect, and give Him the glory. Because the real MVP? It's never been you — it's always been Him.

Apostle Paul speaks to us in 1 Corinthians 15:57,

"But thanks be to God! He gives us the victory through our Lord Jesus Christ."

Your ultimate win is already secured. Jesus is the victory, and you're living in His win.

Call to Action: Let the Headlines Say You Showed Up

You've read the Word. You've fought through the fire. You've stared down the lies. And now — it's time to rise. This world doesn't need more men sitting on the sidelines. It needs *you* — awake, armored, and aligned with Heaven. Make the next chapter of your life headline-worthy.

Show up when others shrink back.

Speak truth when it's easier to stay quiet.

Love fiercely, lead humbly, and walk boldly.

Let your legacy shout louder than your excuses.

You don't need a spotlight to be a story worth telling.

You just need the courage to *live like God is in you.*

Now go — run in such a way as to get the prize.

Make Heaven proud.

Let Hell tremble.

And may every step you take from this day forward carry the weight of this headline:

EXTRA! EXTRA! READ ALL ABOUT IT — A CHAMPION JUST STOOD UP.

CHAPTER 32
EXTRA, EXTRA, READ ALL ABOUT IT

But those who wait on the Lord shall renew their strength; They shall mount up with wings like eagles. They shall run and not be weary, They shall walk and not faint.
— Isaiah 40:31

The phrase **"Extra! Extra! Read all about it!"** originated in the late 19th century, when newspapers would publish "extra editions" to report breaking news outside the regular printing schedule. Young newsboys, often poor or orphaned children, would shout the phrase on street corners to grab attention and boost sales, especially during major events like wars, assassinations, or disasters. It became a cultural symbol of urgency and important headlines.

But not every headline was bad. Sometimes, they shouted with joy — **"Peace Declared! War is Over!," "Yanks Win the Pennant!,"** or **"President Elected!"** When the moment was big and worth celebrating, their voices carried it through the streets.

That same spirit of spreading something too good to keep quiet is exactly how Isaiah 40:28–31 should hit us. It's more than a Bible verse. It's breaking news for the weary, a promise for the discouraged, and a headline of hope that needs to be heard: *God doesn't grow tired, and those who wait on Him will rise up like eagles.* That's not just worth reading — it's worth shouting.

When we believe that, something in us shifts. We stop dragging our feet and start standing tall. We move like men with purpose. We move like the champions we are — not because of our strength, but because of His. That's why Isaiah 40:28-31 is not just worth reading — it's worth shouting.

EXTRA! EXTRA! READ ALL ABOUT IT!

Have you not known?

Have you not heard?

The Lord is the everlasting God, the Creator of the ends of the earth.

He does not faint or grow weary; His understanding is unsearchable.

He gives power to the weak and to those who have no might He increases their strength.

Even youths shall faint and be weary, and young men shall fall exhausted…

…but those who wait for the Lord shall renew their strength.

Let's break this down:

The Lord is the everlasting God, the Creator of the ends of the earth.

That's a reset right there. A reminder of who's really in control.

He does not faint or grow weary; His understanding is unsearchable.

When you run out of answers, He still understands.

He gives power to the weak and to those who have no might He increases strength.

When you feel like quitting, He still has the strength to give.

But understand this: the world may seem heavy at times. You've got bills to pay. You're burned out from working at a job you hate. You're fighting an invisible enemy who wants to steal your focus, your family, and your future. The devil is not playing games. He's coming after your mind with lies, after your marriage with division, and after your purpose with distraction.

This is warfare, not an inconvenience.

That heavy feeling you can't shake? That apathy that creeps in? That sense that you'll never measure up or you're just average? That's not just life — that's a spiritual strategy designed to keep you passive when God called you to be powerful.

The enemy isn't scared of a man who goes to church. He's scared of a man who stands in the gap, lifts up his family, speaks the truth, prays with conviction, and doesn't back down just because it's hard.

It's time.

Armor up.

Get in the Word.

Get around other men who are fighting too.

And stop letting comfort be your king.

You weren't made to coast. You were made to hold the line.

You were made to lead your home, serve your church, and walk into rooms carrying the presence of a living God.

And when you stand up like that, Heaven takes notice. Hell takes notice, too. Because when a man realizes who he is in Christ and starts moving like it, he becomes a dangerous force for the enemy to contend with — not just for himself, but for every generation that comes after him.

Don't just read the Scripture.

Shout it. Live it. Bleed it. Fight for it. Like the champion you are.

Rise up, man of God.

Let the headlines of Heaven declare:

EXTRA! EXTRA! READ ALL ABOUT IT — A CHAMPION JUST STOOD UP.

Reflection Prompt

- Where in your life do you need to adopt a championship mindset?
- Are you leaning into your own strength or allowing the Lord to renew it?
- What would it look like to live like someone who knows they've already been claimed by victory?

Prayer

Father, I don't want to live like I'm defeated when you've called me to be a champion. Help me walk in victory. Give me a mindset that rises above my circumstances. Strengthen me when I'm weary. Remind me of who I am when I forget. Teach me how to lead — not just in public, but behind closed doors, where it matters most. Help me to show up for my family, to fight for what's right, and to walk with boldness and humility. I'm not depending on my own strength — I'm depending on Yours. Make me into the man You designed me to be.

In Jesus' name, Amen.

Pause and Ponder this Scripture – God's Champion Spirit

Do you not know that in a race, all the runners run, but only one gets the prize? Run in such a way as to get the prize. — 1 Corinthians 9:24

Byron Williams with his Grandsons

About the Author

Byron Williams is a former professional wide receiver whose football career spanned 12 seasons across the NFL, CFL, and World League of American Football. Known for his explosive speed and playmaking ability, he made his greatest impact with the New York Giants, after being drafted by the Green Bay Packers in the 10th round of the 1983 NFL Draft. His NFL journey also included time with the Philadelphia Eagles, Indianapolis Colts, and Detroit Lions. Byron continued his career in the Canadian Football League with the B.C. Lions, Ottawa Rough Riders, and Saskatchewan Roughriders, and later competed in the World League with the Orlando Thunder and the New York/New Jersey Knights. No matter the team or the league, Byron left his mark as a fast, fearless, and reliable receiver.

After retiring from professional football, Byron transitioned into the 400m running tracks and turf installations industry, working on athletic fields across schools and communities. But it wasn't just the turf that caught his attention—it was the kids playing on it. He noticed a deeper need: mentorship, encouragement, and guidance for young people striving to find their way. That realization stirred something in him.

In response, Byron founded the Best Wishes Foundation, a nonprofit devoted to youth development through mentorship, education, and

ABOUT THE AUTHOR

community support. For more than 25 years, he has led football camps and leadership programs that go far beyond the game. Byron teaches the fundamentals of football, as well as life-changing lessons in character, discipline, resilience, and integrity. His dedication to empowering the next generation earned him the prestigious Presidential Volunteer Service Award, honoring the profound impact he's made on countless lives. To learn more about the Best Wishes Foundation, visit https://bestwishesfoundation.org.

Byron is also the founder of the Byron Williams Annual Football Camp, which continues to pour into youth through sports and leadership. To learn more, visit www.texasnflflagfootball.com.

A devoted family man and faith-filled leader, Byron lives with God at the center of all he does. His mission is to inspire others to pursue their purpose with integrity, courage, and unwavering belief. Byron is a builder of fields, dreams, and lives. He's a living testament to what's possible when passion, purpose, and faith collide.

Thanking all of my family members, friends, teachers, teammates, church members, fraternity brothers (Kappa Alpha Psi), The NFLPA, and NFL Alumni as well as all of my Coaches, for so many memories, stories, and inspiration ~ lifelong experiences.

www.ingramcontent.com/pod-product-compliance
Lightning Source LLC
Chambersburg PA
CBHW050111170426
43198CB00014B/2530